Mark Beckner
SharePoint Online Development, Configuration, and Administration

W0017949

Mark Beckner

SharePoint Online Development, Configuration, and Administration

—

Advanced Quick Start Guide

ISBN 978-1-5474-1734-6
e-ISBN (PDF) 978-1-5474-0125-3
e-ISBN (EPUB) 978-1-5474-0130-7

Library of Congress Control Number: 2018962042

Bibliographic information published by the Deutsche Nationalbibliothek
The Deutsche Nationalbibliothek lists this publication in the Deutsche Nationalbibliografie;
detailed bibliographic data are available on the Internet at http://dnb.dnb.de.

Published by Walter de Gruyter Inc., Boston/Berlin
Printing and binding: CPI books GmbH, Leck
Typesetting: MacPS, LLC, Carmel

www.degruyter.com

About De|G PRESS

Five Stars as a Rule

De|G PRESS, the startup born out of one of the world's most venerable publishers, De Gruyter, promises to bring you an unbiased, valuable, and meticulously edited work on important topics in the fields of business, information technology, computing, engineering, and mathematics. By selecting the finest authors to present, without bias, information necessary for their chosen topic *for professionals*, in the depth you would hope for, we wish to satisfy your needs and earn our five-star ranking.

In keeping with these principles, the books you read from De|G PRESS will be practical, efficient and, if we have done our job right, yield many returns on their price.

We invite businesses to order our books in bulk in print or electronic form as a best solution to meeting the learning needs of your organization, or parts of your organization, in a most cost-effective manner.

There is no better way to learn about a subject in depth than from a book that is efficient, clear, well organized, and information rich. A great book can provide life-changing knowledge. We hope that with De|G PRESS books you will find that to be the case.

DOI 10.1515/9781547401253-202

Acknowledgments

Thank you to my editor, Jeff Pepper, who has worked with me on so many books. Thanks to Jennifer Curiak for working through each item and verifying the accuracy of things. And thanks to my friend Triston Arisawa who ensured that the web part code in this book was simple and functional. I really appreciate everyone.

DOI 10.1515/9781547401253-203

About the Author

Mark Beckner is an enterprise solutions expert. With over 20 years of experience, he leads his firm Inotek Group, specializing in business strategy and enterprise application integration with a focus in health care, CRM, supply chain and business technologies.

He has authored numerous technical books, including *Administering, Configuring, and Maintaining Microsoft Dynamics 365 in the Cloud, Using Scribe Insight, BizTalk 2013 Recipes, BizTalk 2013 EDI for Health Care, BizTalk 2013 EDI for Supply Chain Management, Microsoft Dynamics CRM API Development*, and more. Beckner also helps up-and-coming coders, programmers, and aspiring tech entrepreneurs reach their personal and professional goals.

Mark has a wide range of experience, including specialties in BizTalk Server, SharePoint, Microsoft Dynamics 365 Silverlight, Windows Phone 7.5, SQL Server, SQL Server Reporting Services (SSRS), .NET Framework, .NET Compact Framework, C#, VB.NET, ASP.NET, and Scribe.

Beckner's expertise has been featured in *Computerworld, Entrepreneur, IT Business Edge, SD Times, UpStart Business Journal*, and more.

He graduated from Fort Lewis College with a bachelor's degree in computer science and information systems. Mark is married to his wife, Sara, and they live in Colorado with their two children, Ciro and Iyer.

DOI 10.1515/9781547401253-204

About the Technical Reviewer

Jennifer Curiak specializes in Dynamics 365 implementations, agile coaching, project management, business analysis, quality assurance, and technical writing. She works to help teams in a variety of industries become more productive, communicate more effectively, and generally get stuff done.

A writer at heart, Curiak started her career as a technical writer for a software company in 2000 and has evolved into designing solutions, managing QA processes and resources, coaching large and small teams in agile development practices, acting as scrum master, and working on Dynamics 365 customizations and implementations. She was the technical reviewer on the book *Administering, Configuring, and Maintaining Microsoft Dynamics 365 in the Cloud, BizTalk: Azure Applications*, and *Power BI Data Analysis and Visualization*, and continues to write in-house technical documentation and end-user documentation, and contributes to other professional publications.

Jennifer and her husband Mike live in Western Colorado and spend most of their free time exploring empty and desolate areas of the West by mountain bike and packraft. She can be contacted directly at jcuriak@inotekgroup.com.

DOI 10.1515/9781547401253-205

Contents

Chapter 1: Licensing, Administration, and Data Migration —— 1
Licensing and the Office 365 Portal —— 1
External Users Licensing (Guest Access) —— 4
User Administration —— 7
SharePoint Administration —— 9
Data Migration —— 12
Usage Reports —— 15
Summary —— 20

Chapter 2: Core SharePoint Online Functionality —— 21
Sites —— 21
Lists —— 26
Pages —— 29
Document Libraries —— 30
Sync Document Libraries —— 33
Basic Document Collaboration —— 34
Setting Permissions —— 35
Tasks, Calendars, and Other Apps —— 38
Summary —— 41

Chapter 3: Styling and Visuals —— 43
Basic Styling —— 43
Creating a Site Based on a Different Template —— 45
Navigation —— 48
Modifying Pages —— 50
Embedding a Document in a Page —— 52
Adding a Chart —— 55
Using Microsoft Forms for Surveys —— 57
Summary —— 60

Chapter 4: Developing Custom Web Parts —— 61
A Few Thoughts on Level of Effort —— 61
Developing a Web Part —— 62
Web Part Code —— 67
Summary —— 74

Chapter 5: Workflows —— 75
Creating a Flow —— 75

Testing the Flow —— **82**
Approval Workflow —— **84**
Managing Flows —— **89**
Summary —— **91**

Index —— **93**

Introduction

My goal in putting together this book is to provide a quick, yet in-depth understanding of the key components of the SharePoint Online world, and an understanding of what it will take to implement them. Additionally, it is my intent that you become familiar with all the critical aspects of SharePoint in as short a time as possible.

In each chapter I have captured the essence of what you will encounter when you proceed with your own SharePoint implementation. I walk you through the specific steps of what it will take to set up and develop components and provide you with an idea of the level of effort and complexity that is required. With visual aids and scoping ideas you will be able to quickly estimate how much work is ahead of you and whether to include these components in your task.

I hope that you find this book a valuable resource, saving you an enormous amount of time and frustration, as you look to implement SharePoint Online within your own environment.

DOI 10.1515/9781547401253-207

Chapter 1
Licensing, Administration, and Data Migration

No matter how familiar you are with past versions of SharePoint, the licensing model and administration of your environment and underlying sites will be new territory. This chapter outlines the steps needed to get your SharePoint instance set up, how to add users, and how to administrate your solutions.

Licensing and the Office 365 Portal

If you have an Office 365 (O365) subscription, you should already have access to SharePoint. There are many different levels of licensing within O365. The individual consumer or small business may use a basic plan, while a larger corporation would use one of the enterprise levels of licensing. Most O365 licenses will have access to SharePoint, and the functionality in these environments is the same. The most noticeable difference are the web parts and controls that are available (enterprise level will have much more access to controls that allow for data reporting, for example).

To gain access to your SharePoint Online instance, go to portal.office.com (if you don't already have an account, you'll need to sign up). Log in to your account and click on the Admin icon, as shown in Figure 1.1.

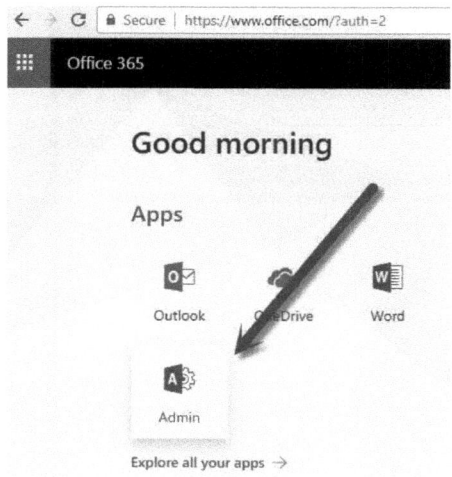

Figure 1.1: The Admin button in the O365 portal

DOI 10.1515/9781547401253-001

In the new window that opens, expand the Users tab and select Active users. You'll see a list of all available user accounts. From here, you can create new users, delete users, and assign licenses. Click on the user that you want to assign a license and permissions to; an additional tab will open with several options (see Figure 1.2).

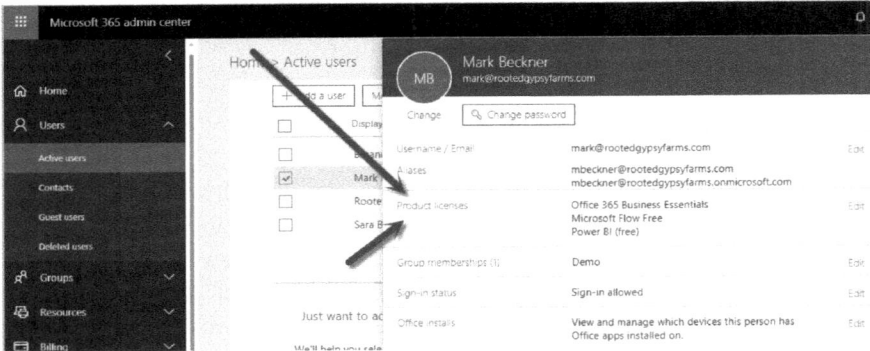

Figure 1.2: Accessing licenses in O365

In the Product licenses section, you can see an overview of what licenses have been assigned. You'll need to click Edit located next to this section to see what is included with your license. After you click Edit, you will see something like what is shown in Figure 1.3. In this example, we show the Office 365 Business Essentials license, which includes everything listed (SharePoint Online as well!). You may also see Microsoft Flow, Power BI, and other licenses that you've added at some point in your Azure development.

∧ Office 365 Business Essentials — On

Stream for Office 365 — On

Office Mobile Apps for Office 365 — On

To-Do (Plan 1) — On

Microsoft Forms (Plan E1) — On

Flow for Office 365 — On

PowerApps for Office 365 — On

Microsoft Teams — On

Microsoft Planner — On

Sway — On

Mobile Device Management for Office 365 (These licenses do not need to be individually assigned) — Off

Office Online — On

Yammer Enterprise — On

Exchange Online (Plan 1) — On

Skype for Business Online (Plan 2) — On

SharePoint Online (Plan 1) — On

∨ Microsoft Flow Free — On
9999 of 10000 licenses available

Figure 1.3: Turning on access to individual apps within the Office 365 Essentials licensing model

You can see a roll-up view of your licensing arrangement by expanding the Billing tab and clicking Licenses (Figure 1.4). This will allow you to quickly determine how many licenses you have and how many have been assigned. If you need additional licenses, you can easily acquire them from within this O365 portal.

Name	Valid	Expired	Assigned
Microsoft Flow Free	10,000	0	1
Office 365 Business Essentials	4	0	4
Power BI (free) What is this?	unlimited	0	1

Home > Licenses — Rooted Gypsy Farms, LLC

Microsoft 365 admin center

Subscriptions
Bills
Payment methods
Licenses
Billing notifications

Figure 1.4: View of active and assigned licenses

External Users Licensing (Guest Access)

By default, you can turn licensing on and set permissions for each user that you have listed in the O365 portal and enable or restrict their access to tools based on this. You also can allow access to SharePoint Online to external users, who are not listed in your list of Users in O365, by invitation or request. This allows you to engage with the external users without having to purchase licenses for them. The value of this option is that organizations that work with outside vendors and the public do not have to purchase licenses for these users.

For example, you may have a company that has licensed O365 users that have full licenses for various products. Your company engages with the public and wants to share certain document libraries for read-only or basic contributions (like uploads). By allowing for external users, you only need to pay for the internal licenses and can allow for unlimited "guests." There is no limit to the number of external users you can invite to your SharePoint sites.

To give permissions to External users (or "guest" users), you must first enable your O365 instance to allow for external sharing. In the main O365 Admin portal, click on the home page and in the search bar type "external." You will see several actions available—click the "Sites external sharing" option, as shown in Figure 1.5. A screen will open where you can set restrictions on external usage and duration of available access for external (in this case "anonymous") users.

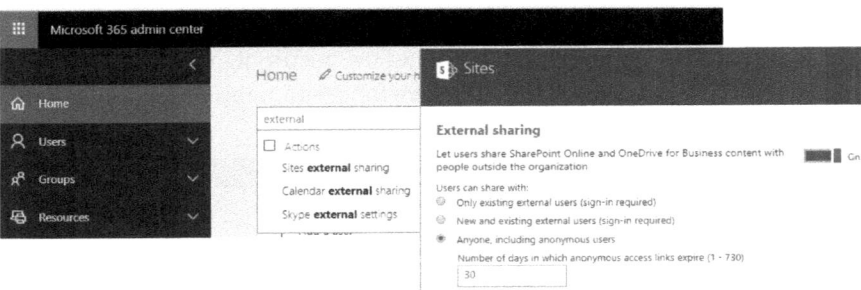

Figure 1.5: O365 External sharing must be enabled to share with external guest users

To give access to external users within SharePoint sites, open a specific site, click the SharePoint settings option in the upper right-hand corner, and click Site permissions (refer to Figure 1.6). Once that has opened, click on Advanced permissions settings. You may also navigate to it from the Site settings page by clicking on Site permissions.

Note: accessing the permissions tab is different when accessing it from a parent site or a subsite.

1. From the parent site, click the Settings icon (upper right corner), select Site settings, then select Site permissions.
2. From a subsite, click the Settings icon (upper right corner), select Site permissions, then select Advanced permissions settings (as Figure 1.6 demonstrates below).

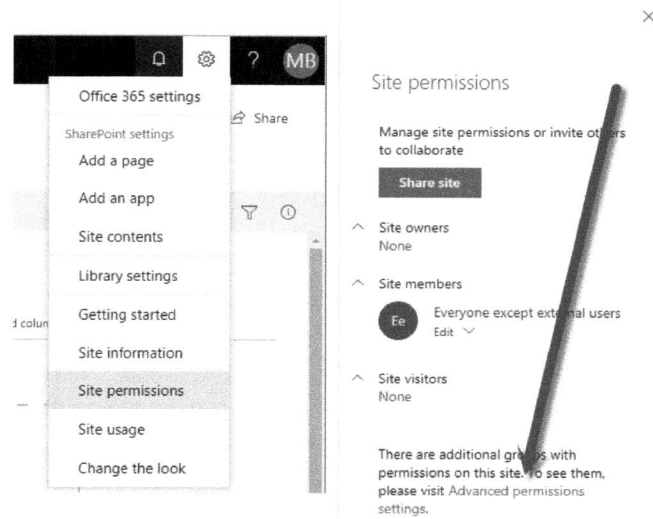

Figure 1.6: Advanced site permissions

In the window that opens, you can click on the "Invite people" tab, or the Grant permissions icon, then type the email address of the person you want to give permissions to. Next, select "Send an email invitation" and then choose a permission level from the drop-down menu. We'll choose "Contribute" permissions for this example (see Figure 1.7)—this will allow the person who is being added to add, update, and delete documents and list items in your site. Of course, any level of access or restriction can be set throughout the site on individual apps and functionality if needed.

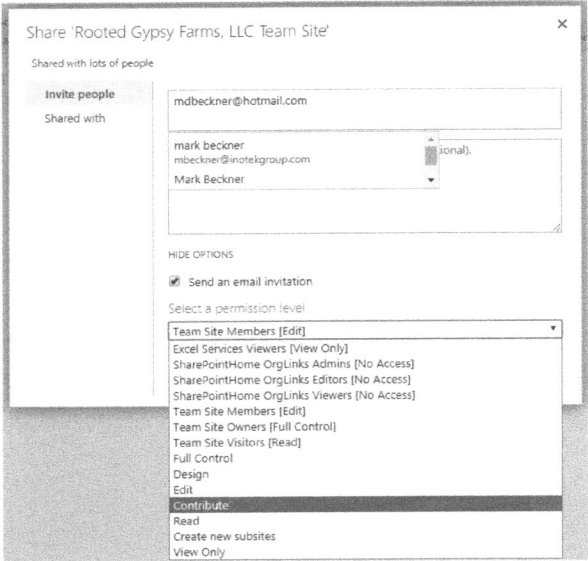

Figure 1.7: Giving Contribute permissions to an external user

When you click the Share button, an email will be sent to the external email address. This email provides a link to the user that will allow them to accept the invitation and access your site. Figure 1.8 shows this invitation as it would appear to an external user. When the invited party clicks this link, they will be asked to log in using an account that has access to Microsoft services. Once the credentials have been entered, they'll be redirected to the site and will be able to work with the content that their security role allows for.

Figure 1.8: External user email invitation

You can monitor the invitations that have been sent and the status of whether they have been accepted within each site. To do this, click on the Site Settings option within a site (in the upper right corner) and then click on the "Access requests and invitations" link. This will open a screen where you can view all pending invitations. Clicking the "History" link will give you an audit trail of all actions that have taken place (see Figure 1.9).

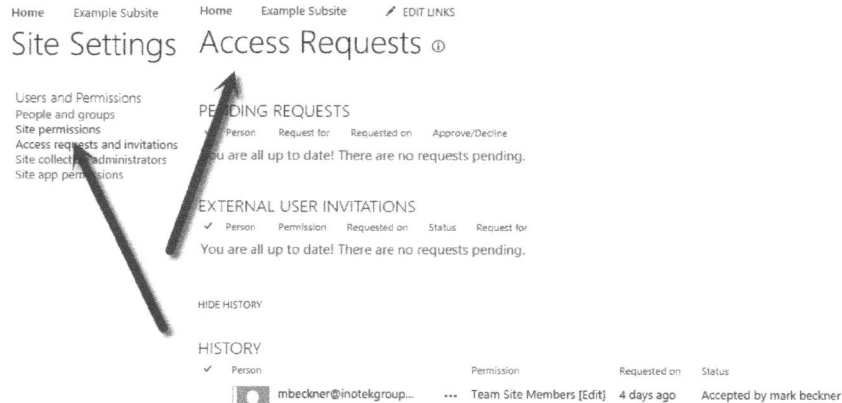

Figure 1.9: A view into pending and accepted invitations

User Administration

All administration associated with users is done at the Office 365 Admin portal level. For example, once an external user has accepted the invitation, that user will be added to the Active users list in your Office 365 portal (see Figure 1.10).

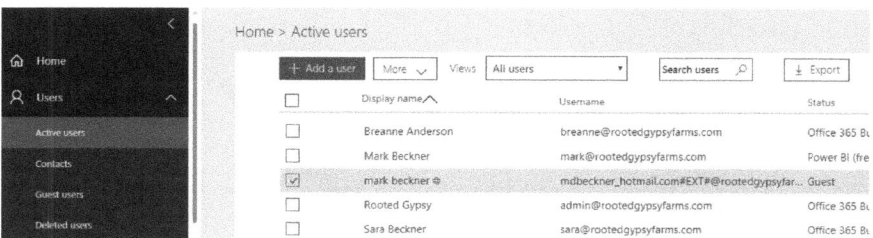

Figure 1.10: All Active users—External users are noted as Guests

Users can be removed from your Active users list. You can delete any user, including external users, by highlighting their entry and selecting "Delete a user." Or, you can click the More menu item on the toolbar and select "Delete a user" (see Figure 1.11). This allows you to easily manage your external accounts and your licensed accounts from a single, central location.

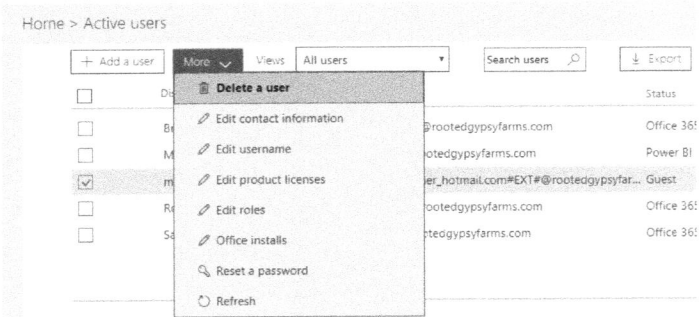

Figure 1.11: Deleting an External user

You may also want to configure security settings for your users, such as whether they can reset their own passwords or share content. Look at the "Security & privacy" tab under Settings in the O365 Admin portal in Figure 1.12 and review the options available. You'll see a link to the Azure AD admin center, which is where even more user-related settings and information can be found (refer to Figure 1.13). Some organizations, when setting up O365, will migrate their local active directory users to the cloud and use this as their primary user management tool.

Figure 1.12: Setting security and privacy properties

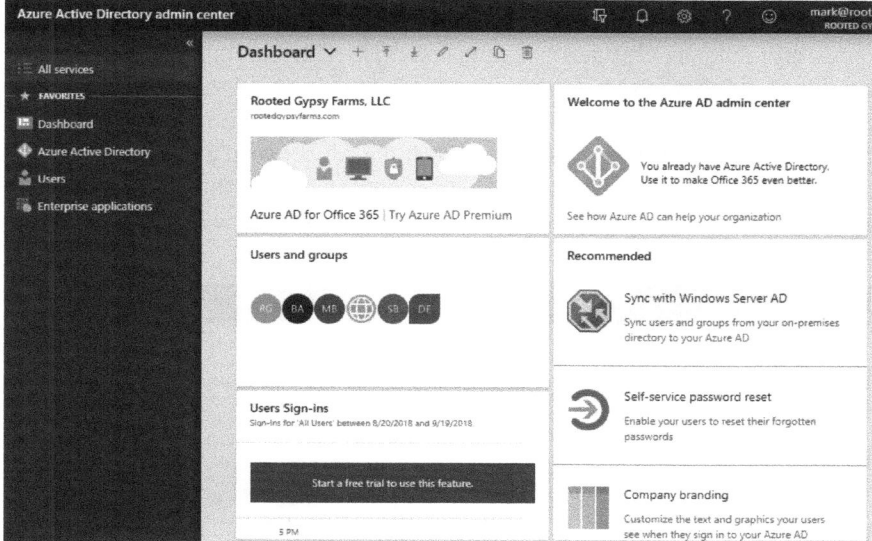

Figure 1.13: Azure Active Directory administration

SharePoint Administration

SharePoint online offers administrators several ways to manage the system as well as providing them with many useful reports and views of the health of the entire system. To access SharePoint administration functionality, expand the Admin centers tab on the left of the Office 365 Admin portal and select SharePoint (see Figure 1.14).

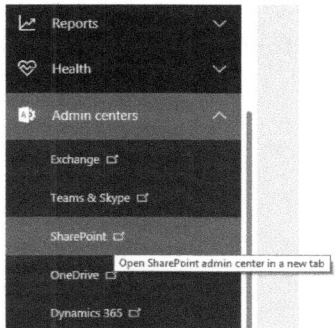

Figure 1.14: Accessing the SharePoint Admin portal

Currently, there are two options for administrating SharePoint: "Classic" admin center and the new "Preview" admin center. The Classic admin center will soon be retired but currently has more functionality than the Preview admin center. The new Admin center is still in "Preview" and has some functionality that the classic one does not. You can toggle back and forth between the classic view and the new view, as you will want to use functionality from both. To access the new view, click the "Try the preview" tab, as shown in Figure 1.15.

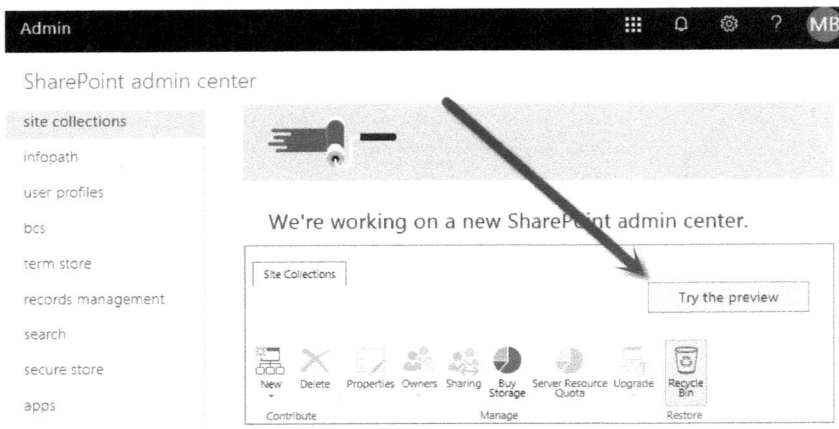

Figure 1.15: Click the "Try the preview" tab to access the new view

The first thing you will notice is the new dashboard. It details current site activity. In the old versions of SharePoint, it was complicated to get a holistic view of your deployed and active sites. Now, with this single dashboard, you can quickly view information about the health and usage of all your sites at once. As you can see in Figure 1.16, information and activity with all the sites is combined in a single level. You can drill down into these reports by clicking the "Details" link in the upper right of the individual reports.

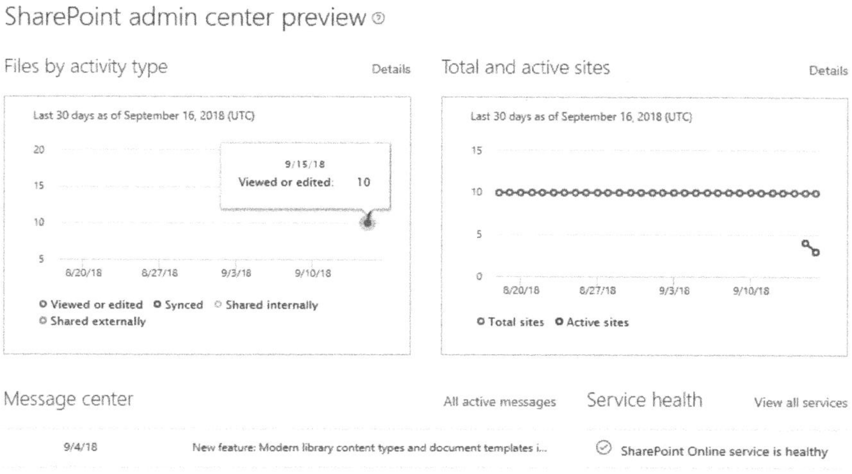

SharePoint admin center preview
Files by activity type
Details
Last 30 days as of September 16, 2018 (UTC)
9/15/18
Viewed or edited: 10
8/20/18
8/27/18
9/3/18
9/10/18
Viewed or edited
Synced
Shared internally
Shared externally
Total and active sites
Details
Last 30 days as of September 16, 2018 (UTC)
Total sites
Active sites
Message center
All active messages
9/4/18
New feature: Modern library content types and document templates i...
Service health
View all services
SharePoint Online service is healthy

Figure 1.16: View activity at the dashboard level

Another useful section in the "Preview" portion of administration is the "Active sites" tab. In Figure 1.17 you can see a report of all the active sites in SharePoint. In this case, there are only two, but for environments where there are dozens of sites being administered, a roll-up view like this is critical. Clicking on an individual site will provide information about the site, such as the URL, the amount of data used, and the amount of activity taking place.

Home
Sites
Active sites
Deleted sites
Settings
Advanced
API management
OneDrive admin center
Data migration
Active sites
Search sites
1 selected
All sites
Site name
Storage used (MB)
Demo
3
Rooted Gypsy Farms, LLC Team Site
2
26 Page views in last 30 days
17 Files viewed/edited in last 30 days
Last activity on September 16, 2018 (UTC)
4 Files / 2 MB Storage used
Properties
Domain
rootedgypsyfarms.sharepoint.com
URL
https://rootedgypsyfarms.sharepoint.com

Figure 1.17: Viewing information about active sites within the SharePoint environment

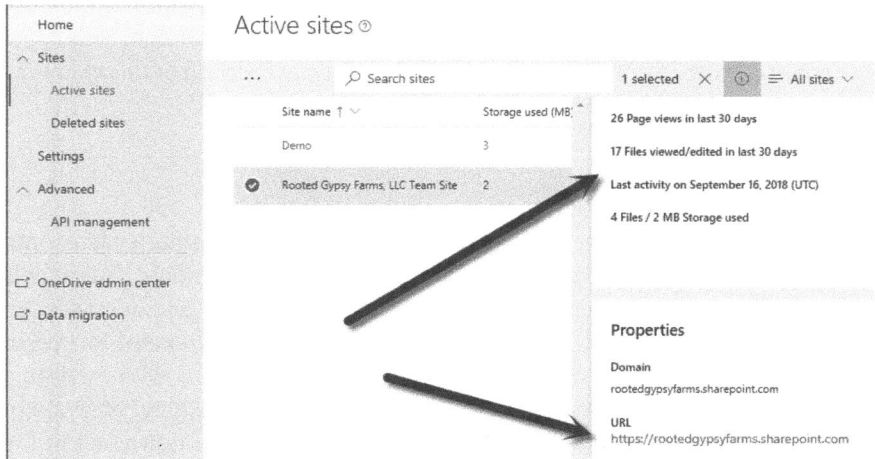

Switching back to the classic view, you'll see that there is considerably more functionality available to you. You'll be most interested in the following functionality, which is accessible from the tabs along the left side of the window:

1. Site collections—displays all sites across your SharePoint implementation and allows you to view information about these sites. Having this single view across your solutions is an invaluable resource, and you'll come back to this page frequently when you have large SharePoint deployments with multiple sites.

2. Search—there is extensive functionality available for configuring search features within your sites. For smaller implementations the default search functionality provided in SharePoint will be adequate, but for more complex solutions—especially ones that contain a large amount of content (like Word documents, PDFs, etc.)—you will likely want to work with custom configurations of your search capabilities.

3. Sharing—if you allow for external sharing (set at the Office 365 portal level), you may want to choose this tab and place restrictions on which users can be invited. Remember, users who have access to your site will be able to invite other users to participate. You may want to restrict invitations and sharing to users that are within specific security groups.

4. Settings—there are several unrelated settings that can be configured on this tab. It is worth your time to choose Settings when you are initiating your sites and see if there is anything particular you want to configure. For example, you may not want any users to be able to create sites—the easiest thing to do is to turn off site creation functionality in this area (under Site Pages).

5. Data migration—this section allows you to migrate data from on-premise SharePoint instances or from file shares to SharePoint Online. This topic requires further explanation, as outlined in the next section of this chapter.

Data Migration

In older editions of SharePoint the migration of data from other sources into SharePoint was done primarily with third-party software and tools. These tools (like Metalogix, as an example) still have a place for complex migration scenarios, but the out of the box migration capabilities of the SharePoint Migration Tool provided with your subscription are useful. To get started with migrating documents, click on the data migration tab within the Classic SharePoint Admin center (see Figure 1.18). Clicking the Install tan will initiate a download of the application, which needs to be installed locally.

Figure 1.18: Data migration

When the application runs after download, you'll see the splash screen and be allowed to sign in. Once you sign in, you'll be able to select the source of your data (see Figure 1.19). For this discussion, we'll select the File Share option. Browse to a folder that you want to migrate and select the Next button in the application.

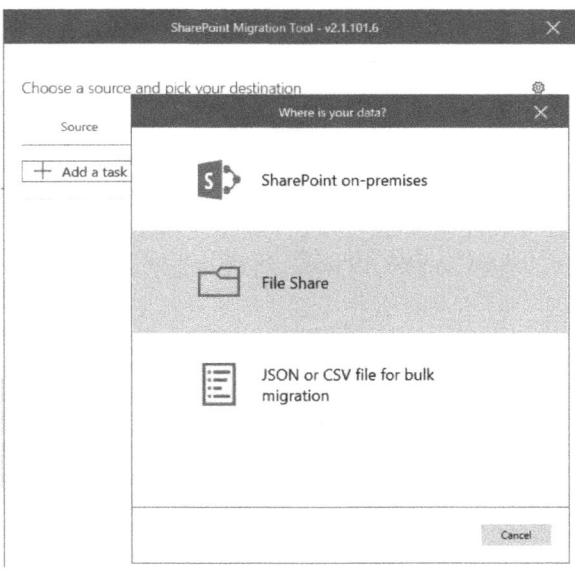

Figure 1.19: Selecting a File Share as the source of your data

Next, select the destination document library you want to migrate your data to. You'll need to enter in the site URL—you just need the root of the URL, do not include anything after "sharepoint.com" (like /SitePages/Home.aspx or similar). After you enter a valid URL, you'll then be able to select the target document library from a drop-down menu. Figure 1.20 shows the source and destination configured. After selecting the destination, click the Add tab.

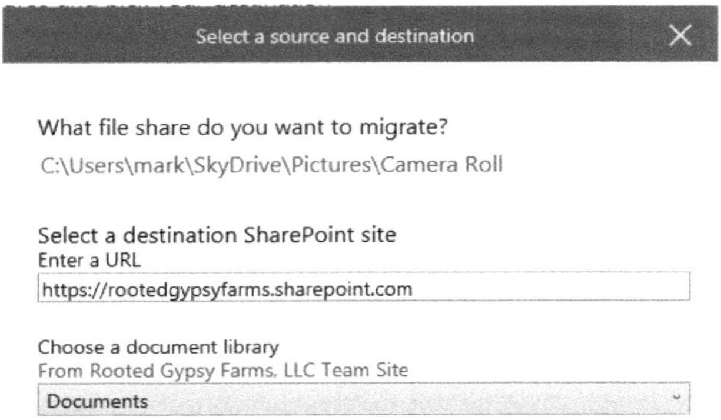

Figure 1.20: Selecting the source and destination for migration

You can add additional folders to migrate by clicking the "Add a task" link, or you can move forward with executing your migration. To migrate your data, click the Migrate tab. A status indicator will show the progress of the migration (see Figure 1.21). Once complete, you'll see your migrated content in the targeted library in SharePoint Online. If your migration fails, the migration tool creates several reports that you can review to determine the cause of failure. The most common cause of failure is permissions—either your user doesn't have access to the source data or the targeted document library has restrictions on it for what content can be uploaded.

Note that you will want to turn off any notifications you might have on the target document library before you upload your data. If you don't, you (and other users) may get a notification for every file that you migrate.

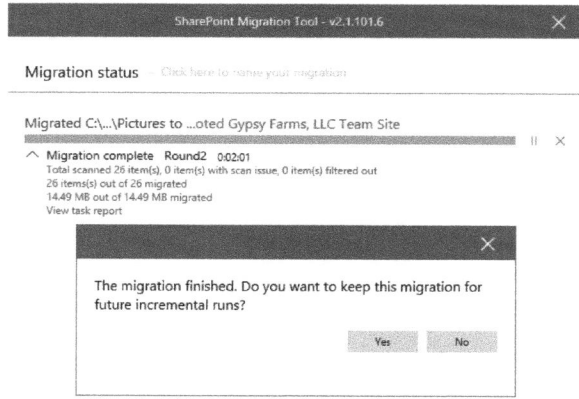

Figure 1.21: Migration progress

When you examine the migrated data you'll notice several things in regard to your files (refer to Figure 1.22 for reference).

1. Modified By is set to the generic "BUILTIN\administrators" user (as opposed to the user that you had logged into the migration tool with).
2. The Modified date is set to the actual date on the original source file or folder.

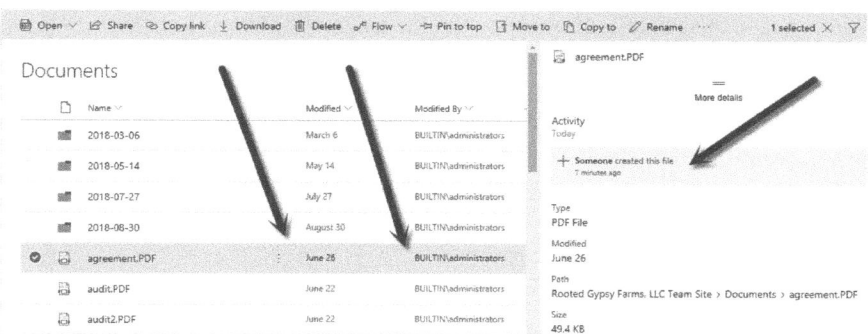

Figure 1.22: Properties on the migrated data

Usage Reports

Clicking on Usage under the Reports tab in the O365 Admin portal lets you review who is accessing SharePoint and how often. You can also see other details that may be of interest, such as how many files have been uploaded and whether content is being edited, along with other information about applications unrelated to SharePoint, but within the O365 domain. Figure 1.23 is an example of this usage dashboard report.

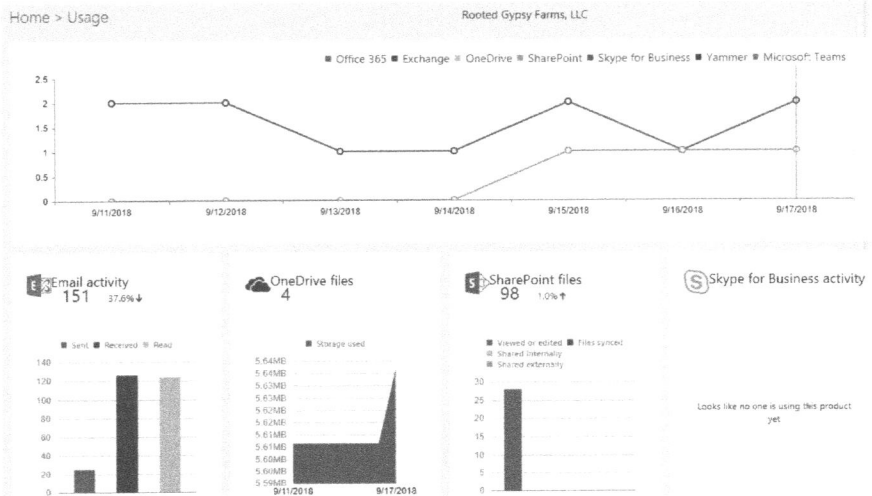

Figure 1.23: Usage reporting

You can also view details about specific site usage. Within a site click the Settings icon, then choose Site Settings. Within a Subsite, click the Settings icon, then select Site usage. Figure 1.24 shows this option along with several of the reports that you can view. Being able to track what documents are the most popular across your document libraries, how many people are visiting your site, and other similar features is critical information for supporting active sites.

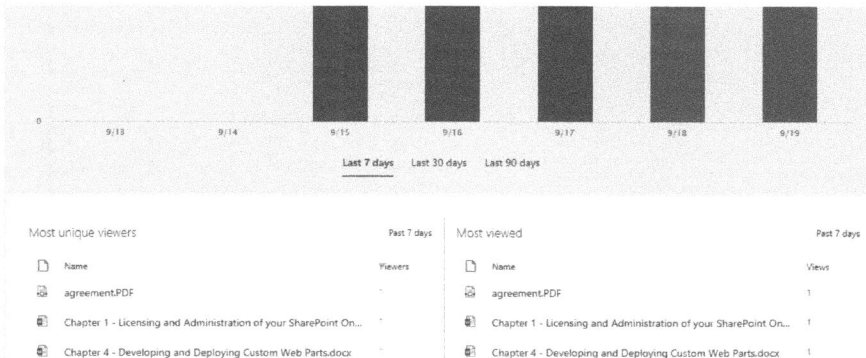

Figure 1.24: Usage reporting

Additionally, you may want to track activity by user. For example, you may want to see what users have deleted content from the site, or who has edited a list. To report on auditing you must first enable it—this can be done by going to Site Settings within a site and clicking on the "Site collection audit settings" link (see Figure 1.25).

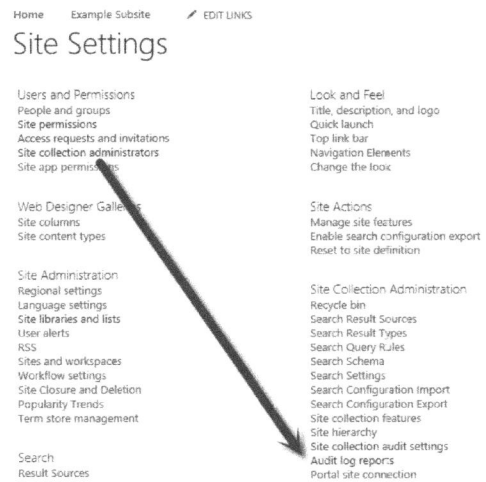

Figure 1.25: Audit settings and audit reports

You can enable tracking on document libraries, documents within those libraries, lists, and sites. Once you have configured the settings the way you want, click the OK button. Figure 1.26 shows all the settings on this screen.

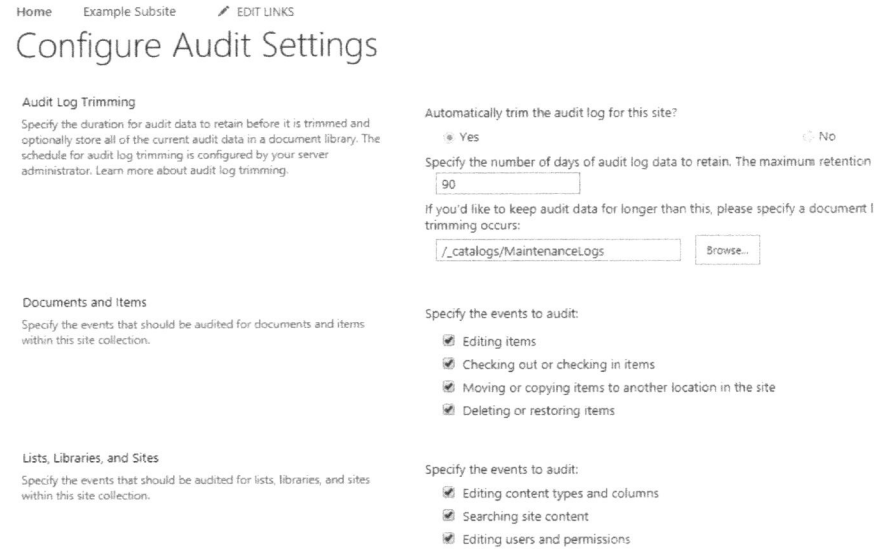

Figure 1.26: Audit settings and audit reports

With auditing turned on, you will now be able to view several reports. Click on the "Audit log reports" link in Site Settings. A list of available reports will be shown, along with a link at the bottom of the screen allowing you to build custom reports. Strangely, all these reports are Excel based, and when you run them you will be required to specify where to export them. For example, clicking on the Content Modifications report (which shows all the content that has been modified during a specific period) opens the screen shown in Figure 1.27. Clicking the Browse tab allows you to select a target to export it to, but this target is limited to locations within SharePoint itself.

Run Reports › Customize Report ⊙

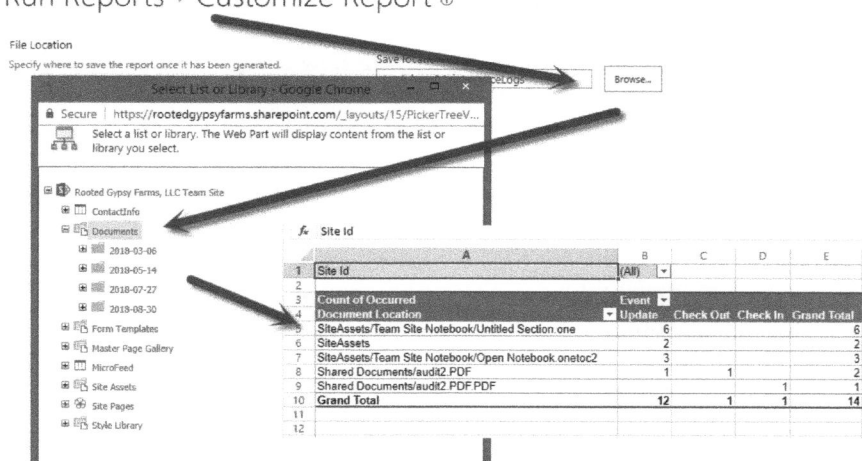

Figure 1.27: Running a report requires that you export an Excel doc to a location within SharePoint

Finally, another area where you can view usage information is from the "Popularity and Search Reports" link on the Site Settings page. Clicking on this link will provide you with several additional Excel based reports (see Figure 1.28) that can be used to gain insight into how your SharePoint sites are being used and how data is being shared.

View Usage Reports ⊙

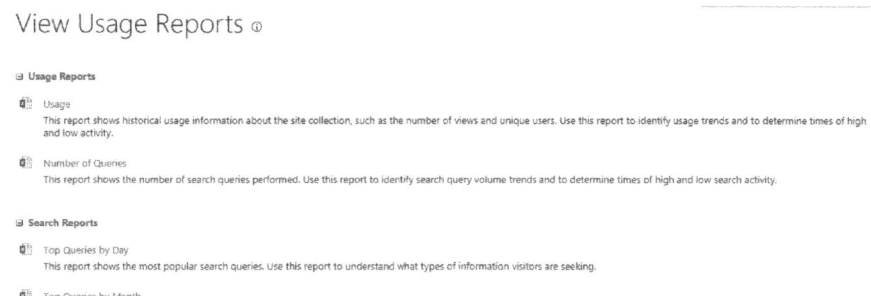

Figure 1.28: Additional usage reports

Summary

At this point, you should have familiarity with how to log into your SharePoint instance, how to give permissions and set security, how to administrate your solutions, and how to perform simple data migrations. You also now have information on how to view a variety of reports that will give you information about how your data is being used and who is accessing it. You have many options to manage users, sites, and your overall SharePoint infrastructure, but your key takeaway should be that it is relatively easy to gain a deep level of insight about what is going on. In addition, you can always add a Power BI solution on top of your SharePoint instance for deep business intelligence!

Chapter 2
Core SharePoint Online Functionality

Now that you know how to access and administer your SharePoint environment, it's time to look at building out sites and all the components within a site! The structure of how these components are set up and configured will be familiar to you if you've worked with SharePoint in the past. We'll work through the basics of setting things up and look at advanced ways of working with these components.

Sites

A site is a container for all other SharePoint component types. To share content, add web parts, create document libraries, and do anything else, you must first create a site. And, in turn, a site must be included in a site collection. To create a site, you can either add it to an existing default site collection or create a new one. For the example shown in Figure 2.1, we will navigate to the site collections tab by clicking on the SharePoint admin center under Admin centers in the O365 portal.

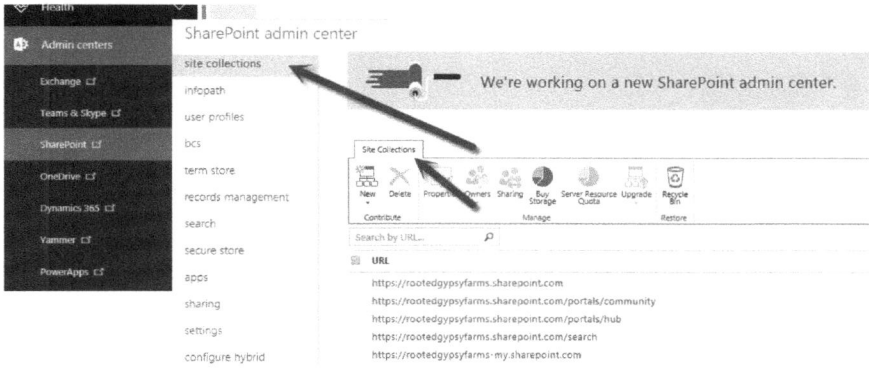

Figure 2.1: Accessing site collections

Clicking on one of the existing site collections (as shown in Figure 2.2) displays information about the site—most importantly, the base URL used to access it. At this level, the number of subsites and the amount of storage used are also helpful to see. From this window, click on the Web Site Address to open the base level site collection in a new tab.

DOI 10.1515/9781547401253-002

site collection properties

Title	Rooted Gypsy Farms, LLC Team Site
Web Site Address	https://rootedgypsyfarms.sharepoint.com/
Primary Administrator	Company Administrator
Administrators	Company Administrator
Number Of Subsites	1
Storage Usage	0.00 GB
Resource Usage	0 resources
Server Resource Quota	300 resources
Resource Usage Warning Level	255 resources

Figure 2.2: Site collection properties

A site collection can consist of one or multiple sites (which are called subsites). When your site has been opened (you can bookmark this URL as the top-level site collection), click on the settings icon in the upper right and then select Site settings from the menu (see Figure 2.3).

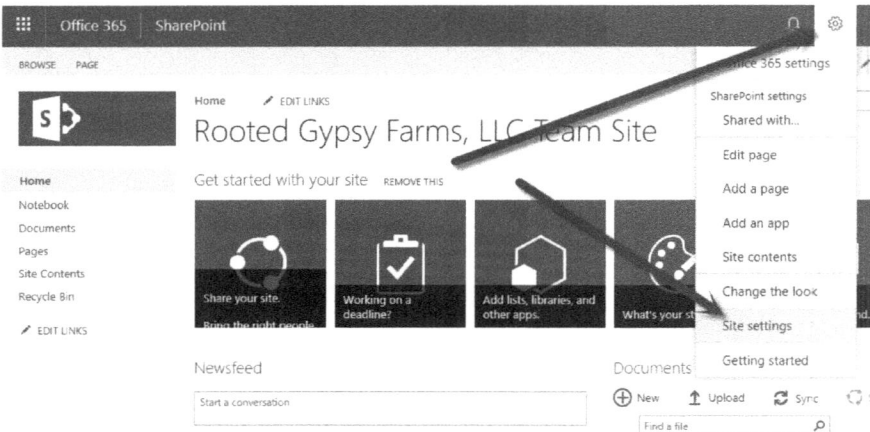

Figure 2.3: Accessing Site settings

The Site settings window that opens gives you access to virtually everything you can do to administratively control the content of your site (including creating new subsites). Under the Site Administration heading, you can click Site libraries and lists. In the next window that opens, click the "Create new content" link. Finally, in the next screen, click on the New tab and select Subsite. This flow is shown in

Figure 2.4. You'll then be able to enter in all the information related to your new subsite. This information includes:

- Name and Description—standard reference information here. Remember that users will be able to directly navigate here, so give your subsite a name that will allow for additional sites.
- Website Address—this is the actual URL that will result from your site naming.
- Template Selection—when you create a site or subsite, you can base it on existing templates. These templates will structure your site for various uses. You should experiment with the different template types to see what you'd like to use. The most common would be a Document Center (used mainly for sharing document content) and a Team Site (used for working collaboratively with others across multiple component types).
- Permissions—you can inherit permissions from the parent site (most common), or you can set your own permissions at the subsite level. The latter option is useful when you want users to be able to access the subsite but not the parent site or other sites in the hierarchy.
- Navigation—which details where the site is accessible from. Sometimes you'll want to be able to supply a link to a subsite from the navigation bar on your parent site, and sometimes you'll only want users to navigate to the site via a URL.

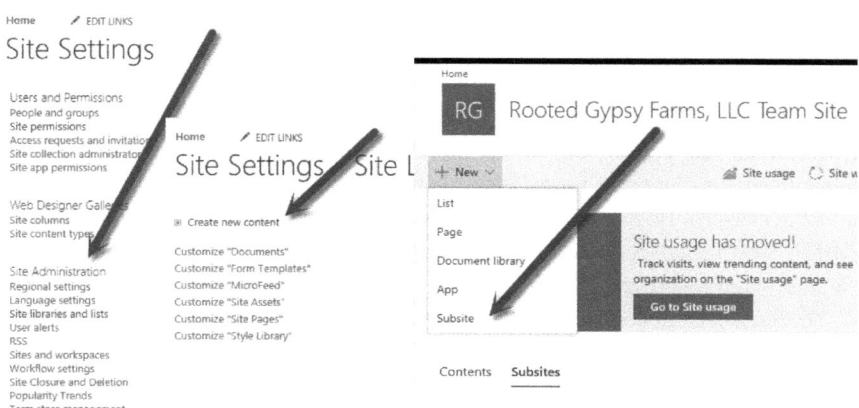

Figure 2.4: Creating a subsite

When you create your subsite (by clicking the Create tab at the bottom of the site creation screen), you'll now be able to browse to it from the parent site (assuming you allowed for that in your navigation settings) and you'll also see that you have an additional count in your top-level site collection properties. Figure 2.5 shows the parent site with the newly created subsite (named in this image "Example Subsite") and the increased count on the subsite properties.

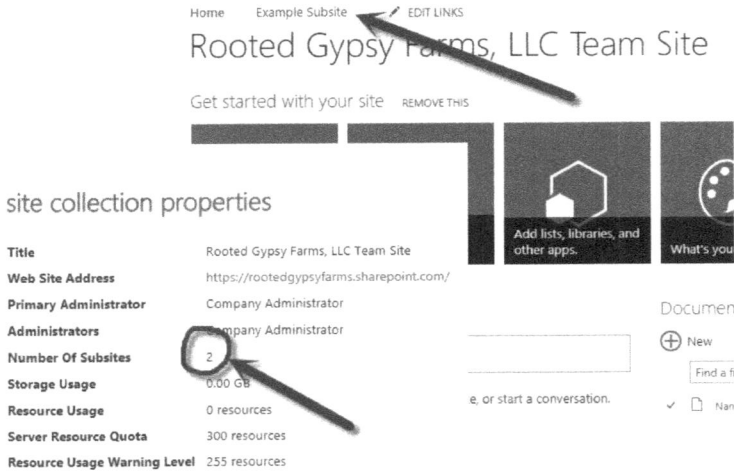

Figure 2.5: Subsite has been added

A site comes with several default configurations that will allow you to begin using it immediately. For example, if you want to share documents, you can click on the Documents tab in your site. If you want a repository of web pages to house information, you can upload them directly to the Pages directory (most commonly used for company knowledge bases where shared read-only information can be accessed). However, you will usually want to customize your site and add controls and functionality that isn't included with the base template you have selected when creating your site.

To demonstrate adding an app to your site, click on the Home tab and then select the "Add lists, libraries, and other apps" icon. Alternatively, if the "Add lists, libraries, and other apps" icon is not available, click the Settings icon (upper right corner), and select Add an app. This will open a screen like that shown in Figure 2.6. There are many apps listed in the Site contents page, so you'll have to scroll through and experiment with adding different ones to see what you are interested in including.

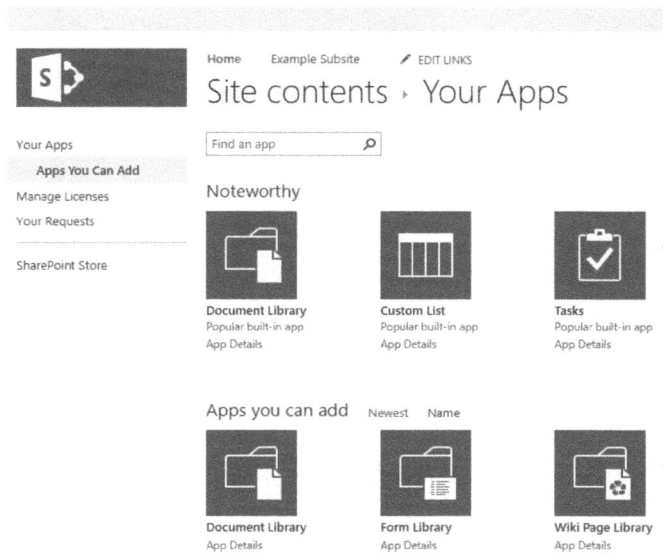

Figure 2.6: The list of apps available to add to your site

As noted above, you can add apps to your site by clicking the Settings icon and then selecting Add apps. You can also add apps and control the content of your SharePoint page by clicking the Edit button in the upper right corner of the site or subsite page. See Figure 2.7.

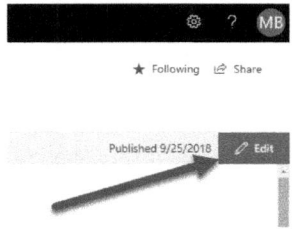

Figure 2.7: Clicking Edit button to edit your site

Clicking the Edit button puts your site into edit mode. You can add or remove apps by hovering your cursor over the border of two web parts and clicking the + button (see Figure 2.8).

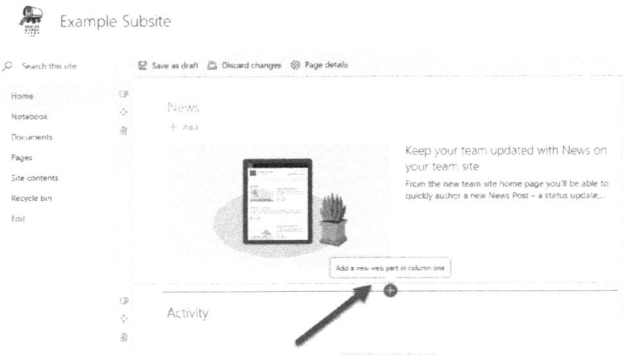

Figure 2.8: Adding web-parts to your site

This allows you to add a section or columns in which to add apps. After adding web parts to your site, click Publish to make your changes available to users.

Lists

Let's look at adding a new list. A list is a collection of information that is not a document or the like, that you may want to store. For example, let's say you have a web page that requires people to fill in details like their name, address, and other contact information. You could create a list in SharePoint to store the records that are saved by the many users who access this contact information page. Each time someone saves their data on the page, that data could be saved to the list. You can access the list in SharePoint to see what information has been entered.

Advanced SharePoint development often uses lists in the same way that SQL tables would be used to share and reference data. Make sure and look through the discussion in Chapter 4 about building a simple Power Apps form based on a list to understand the steps involved in making an interactive form for users to enter data.

To create a list, click on the Custom List icon in the "Your Apps" window that you just opened in the previous section and enter a name for your list, as shown in Figure 2.9.

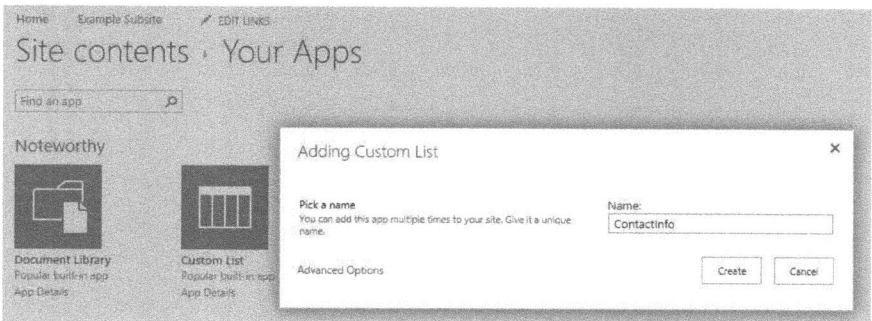

Figure 2.9: Creating a new list

When you click the Create tab, your list will be created and appear under the Site contents tab on your site. When you browse to it, you'll see that it currently has 0 items in it (refer to Figure 2.10). Click on the list to open it.

Figure 2.10: The list is now accessible

When the list opens, you'll see that you can easily create columns. Creating columns requires that you first select the type of column (numeric, string, etc.), then name it. Figure 2.11 shows what the creation of a multiple-choice column looks like. It is quick and simple to create, and you can model out your list structure rapidly. In the case of a contact form as shown in Figure 2.11, you can create columns to handle the structure of your contact information in a matter of minutes.

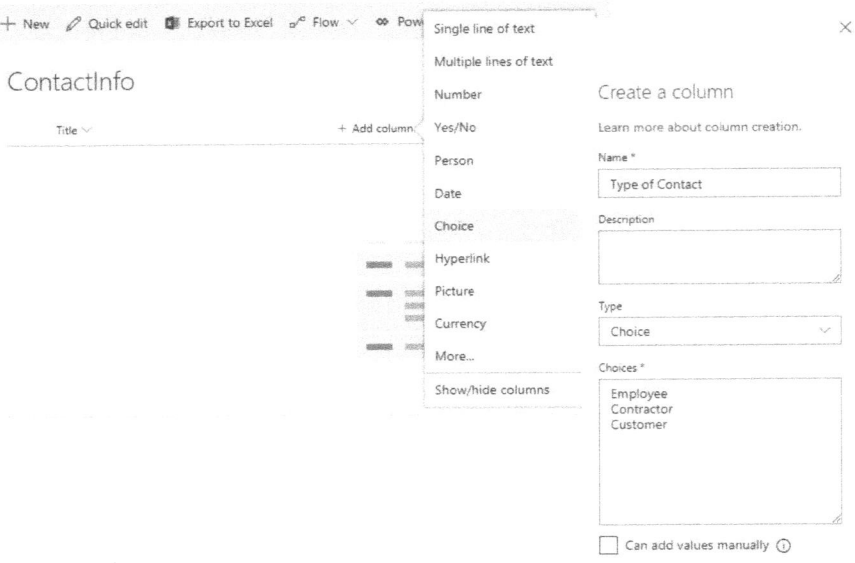

Figure 2.11: Creating a new column on a list

Once you have created columns, you can then add a record by clicking the New button and filling in the information. You may want to use the Quick edit tab to add/edit records within a grid interface. You can alter the columns in your view in the Quick edit grid by clicking the All Items drop-down menu in the upper right of the list control and selecting Edit current view. Figure 2.12 shows these options.

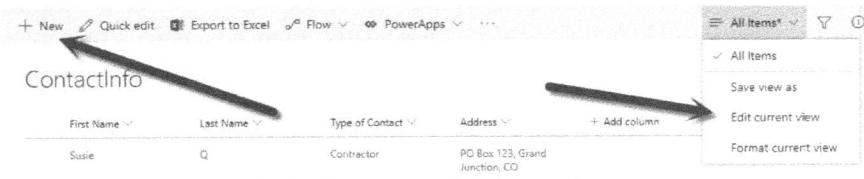

Figure 2.12: Adding records and editing the columns in the current view

Pages

Pages are containers of viewable functionality within your SharePoint site. If you want to give a URL to a user that directs them to a custom web page that has controlled content, you can create a page (rather than just allowing them to click through the default site that was set up during creation). A page can contain text, images, list previews, custom web parts, and a wide variety of other apps and tools. To create a page, click Site Content in your site's navigation menu and then click New from the upper toolbar menu and select Page. This will open a window where you can type in a name for your page and then begin to add content. To add content, click the plus button below the title frame and select from the list of app options. Figure 2.13 shows this page, along with several components that can be added.

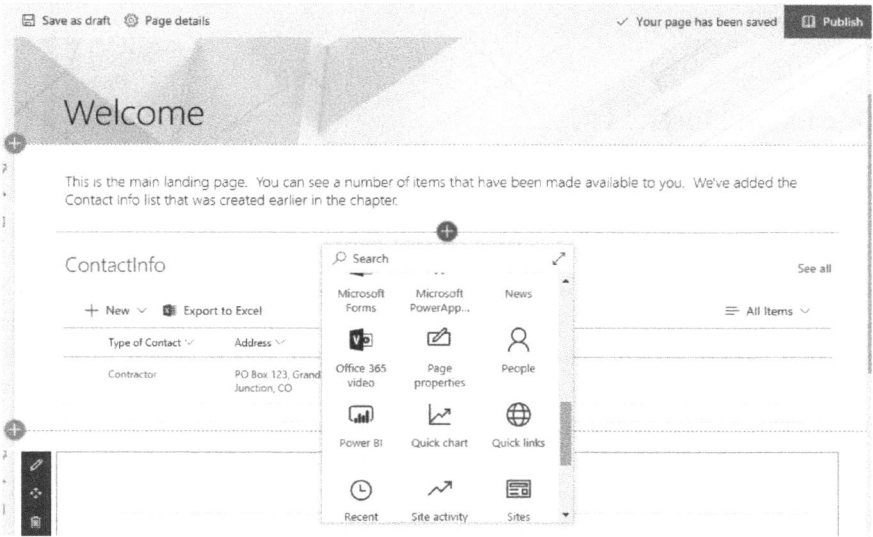

Figure 2.13: Creating a page

Clicking the Publish tab will allow you to make the page available to users. You can allow users to browse to it directly via a URL that you share with them. You can also choose to have it accessible on the site's navigation menu. Figure 2.14 shows the publish window on the left followed by what the published content on the navigation bar looks like.

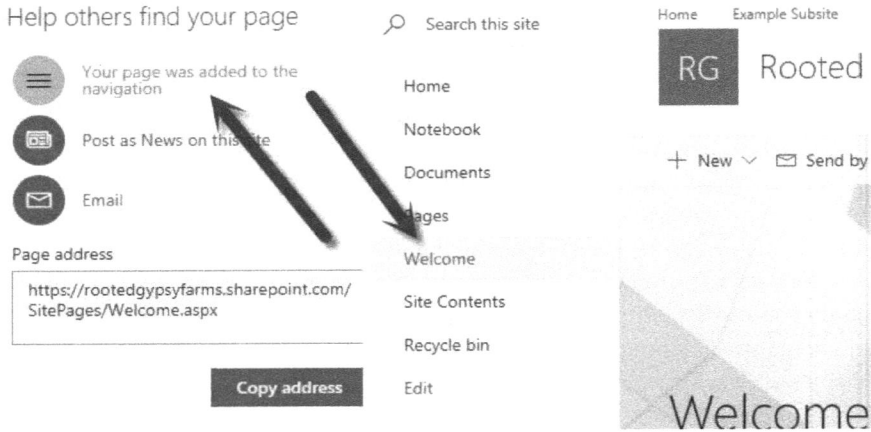

Figure 2.14: Publishing the page allows you to add it to the navigation menu and access it directly via URL

Document Libraries

The ability to share documents and collaborate with multiple users as well as keep an audit history of who has made changes is an essential aspect of Share-Point. When a site is created there is a default Documents directory already set up for you. You may want to create your own directory (this can be done using the Site Contents link, just like we did with the new Page we created), but for this example we'll use the default. Click on the Documents link in your site. You can drag and drop files into this folder to begin working with content. In Figure 2.15 you can see that several files have been added to this document library.

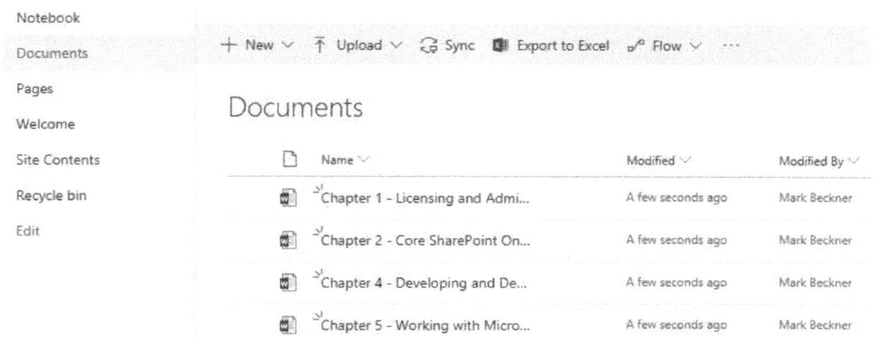

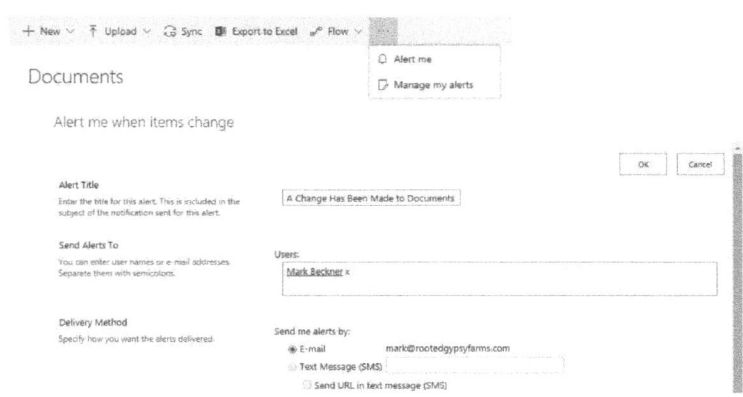

Figure 2.15: Adding documents to the library

You can now create an alert to notify you when a new document is added or an existing document is modified. To do this, click the ellipses on the toolbar and select "Alert me." Configurations related to the alert can be set and the alert saved. Figure 2.16 shows how easy it is to set up an alert. Once you click OK, you will get a notification (email or text, depending on what you have configured) saying that you've set up alerts.

Figure 2.16: Setting up an alert

If you want to view the alerts that you have enabled or you want to turn off an alert, click the "Manage my alerts" option in the same drop-down menu where "Alert me" is. This will open a screen like that shown in Figure 2.17. Here you can view existing alerts, add new ones, and delete outdated ones.

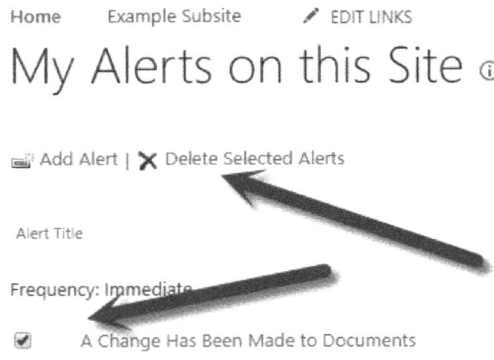

Figure 2.17: Managing alerts

The amount of functionality that is tied to individual documents is extensive. Clicking on the context menu next to any of the uploaded documents shows the wide variety of items that are available to you. Looking at the basics of collaboration and history tracking, Figure 2.18 shows the option for opening the document in Word Online. Selecting this will open the document in a browser version of Word. Depending on the permissions assigned to the user, the document can be read or edited in this window. As revisions are made, the data is automatically saved back to SharePoint.

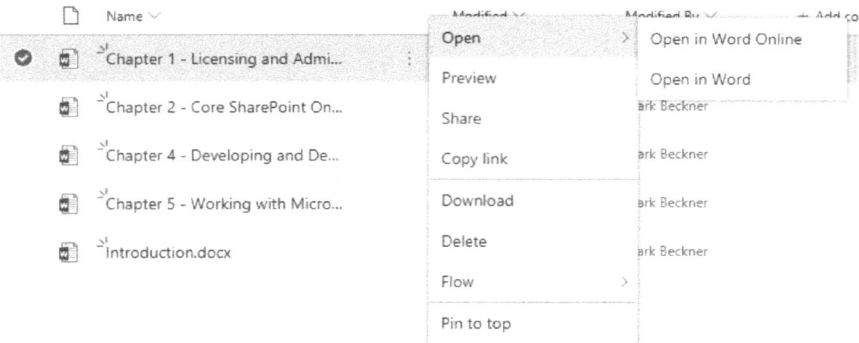

Figure 2.18: Opening a document

If you set up alerts, you'll get an email when a change is made. If you select Version history from the context menu on your document, you'll be able to see the history of changes made. Figure 2.19 shows this version history and notification on one of the documents.

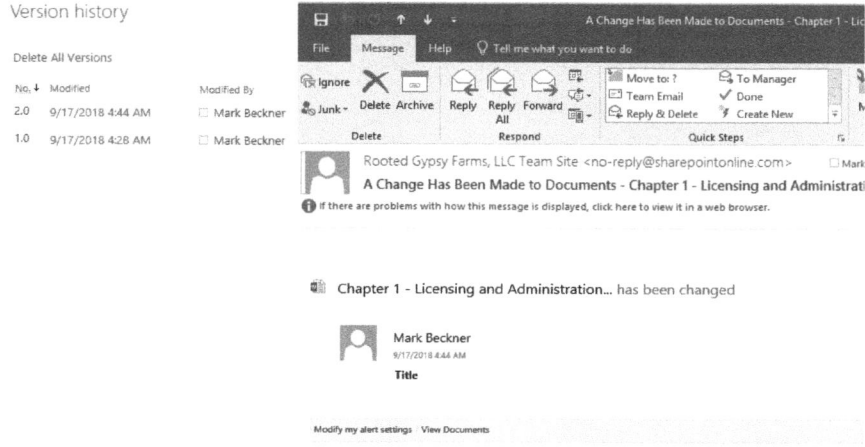

Figure 2.19: Version history updated and notification sent as changes are made

If a user wants to work with the document for an extended period of time, they can select "Check Out" from the context menu, which will lock the document from other users. Once done working on the document, the user can click the "Check In" option from the menu. Many other actions are available to users such as triggering workflows when certain conditions are met. See Chapter 5 for discussions around triggered custom workflows.

Sync Document Libraries

If you would like to work with your document library locally, you can click the Sync tab on the toolbar. When chosen, a dialogue box will pop up allowing you to configure a location in OneDrive. As you can see in Figure 2.20, you can select which files and folders to sync with OneDrive. Once you have completed this configuration, the OneDrive folder will be set up and you'll be able to treat this folder just like any other local folder on your computer. Documents added to the folder will be uploaded to SharePoint. As items are added to the SharePoint library, they will simultaneously be downloaded to your local folder.

This is great functionality when you are working with a lot of your own content. If you are in an environment where documents are being revised by multiple users, and you are collaborating, you should use the "Check In" and "Check Out" functionality directly in SharePoint Online so that no content history is lost.

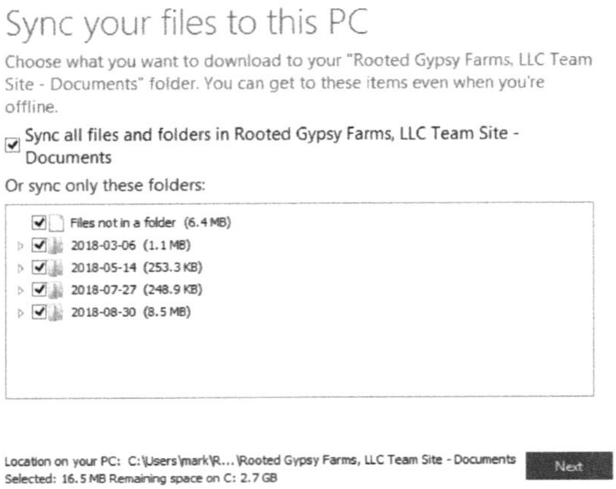

Sync your files to this PC

Choose what you want to download to your "Rooted Gypsy Farms, LLC Team Site - Documents" folder. You can get to these items even when you're offline.

☑ Sync all files and folders in Rooted Gypsy Farms, LLC Team Site - Documents

Or sync only these folders:

- ☑ Files not in a folder (6.4 MB)
- ▷ ☑ 2018-03-06 (1.1 MB)
- ▷ ☑ 2018-05-14 (253.3 KB)
- ▷ ☑ 2018-07-27 (248.9 KB)
- ▷ ☑ 2018-08-30 (8.5 MB)

Location on your PC: C:\Users\mark\R...\Rooted Gypsy Farms, LLC Team Site - Documents   Next
Selected: 16.5 MB Remaining space on C: 2.7 GB

Figure 2.20: Choosing which documents and folder to sync

Basic Document Collaboration

The ability to collaborate on documents is the oldest SharePoint function. There is a lot of functionality built into Microsoft Office products that ties in this SharePoint collaboration option, and you'll see it when you check-out a document and work on it in Word, Excel, or other editing applications. The standard flow for document collaboration is:

1. If you want to lock the file while you work on it, click on the context menu of a Word document (for example) and select More and then Check Out. Make sure and check it back in once you are done editing!

2. Next, click Open and then select Word (or Excel, etc.). If you want to simplify things, or you don't have Office installed locally on your computer, you can select the Online version of the Office product you are trying to open.

3. You can now edit your document. If you are using Word, and you save, it will automatically be saved to SharePoint, creating a new version.

4. If you have the document checked-out, and someone else opens it, they will see the warning message shown in Figure 2.21 and will not be able to edit the file.

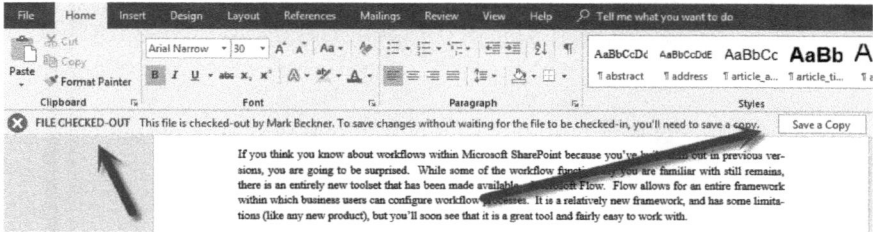

Figure 2.21: This document has been checked-out by another user and can't be edited

5. After saving your edits, close the document and check the file back in (open the context menu, select More, then select Check In).

Setting Permissions

To give users access to your site, you must assign them security rights. These rights may be as simple as giving everyone the same access to all components and apps within the site or as complex as setting permissions on each individual object that has been created. You may have a group of users that you want to give full permissions across the site to, while another group needs to only be able to work with content in a specific document library. Giving access to users is easy and can be done at several levels. Some of the most common are:

1. From virtually any app, site, or component, you can click the Share button in the upper right corner and indicate who you would like to invite to this area of your solution. By clicking the Show Options link on the screen that pops up (see Figure 2.22) you can set the permission level to a specific group.

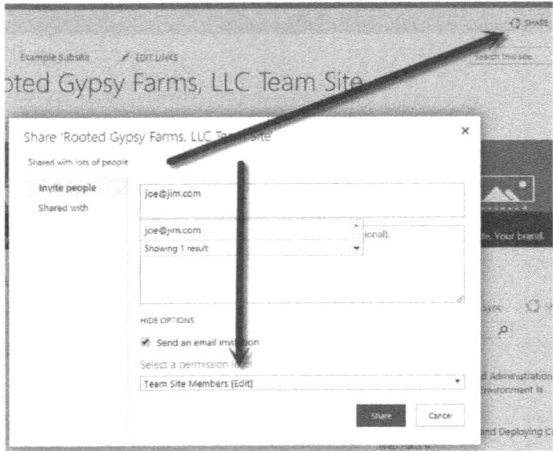

Figure 2.22: Using the Share button at the site level

2. For more comprehensive permission administration, click the Site Settings icon on the main site screen, click "Site permissions," then click the Advanced permissions settings (at the very bottom of the Site permissions tab). The permissions screen will open (see Figure 2.23).

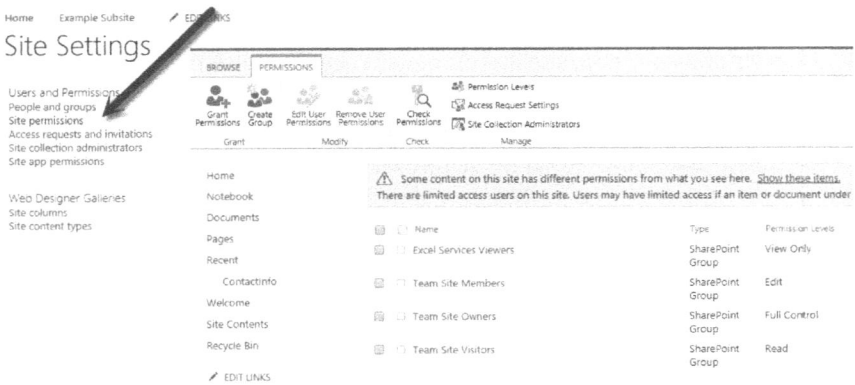

Figure 2.23: Using the Share tab at the site level

From this permissions screen you can click on the following (note that some of the available tabs may change based on whether you are at the top-level site or whether you are within a subsite):

a. Grant Permissions—this is the same functionality and dialogue box that is available from the previous step, allowing for sharing of the site with specific users.

b. Create Group—this lets you create a new group with specific permissions. You can add users to this group and then assign this group permissions to specific objects.

c. Edit and Remove Permissions—this allow you to manage existing permissions.

d. Check Permissions—you can click this tab to search for users or groups and see what access they have (see Figure 2.24).

Figure 2.24: Checking a specific user's permissions

3. You can share individual documents by clicking the context menu next to the document and selecting Share (see Figure 2.25).

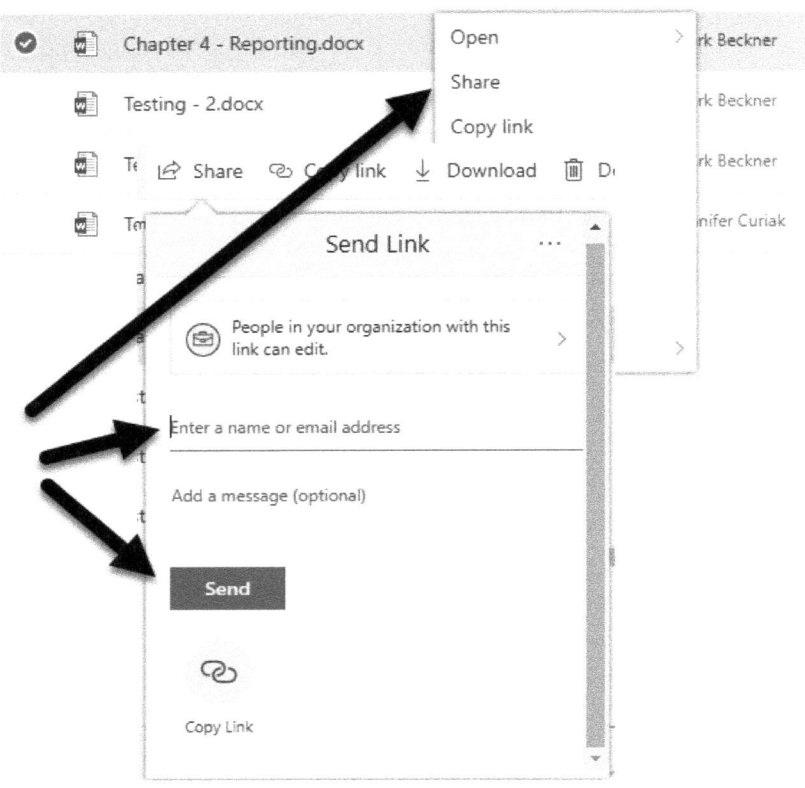

Figure 2.25: Sharing an individual document

Tasks, Calendars, and Other Apps

There are additional controls that you'll want to take note of, as they are very common across SharePoint implementations. These controls include tasks, calendars, discussion boards, news feeds, etc. They can be added to a variety of places, one of which is to browse to the Home tab in your site and select the "Add lists, libraries, and other apps" icon. This will give you access to the most common controls. You can certainly write your own as well—look at Chapter 4 on how to do this!

If the "Add lists, libraries, and other apps" icon is not visible, at a site or subsite page you can click the Settings icon, then select Add an app.

We'll look up the Task app to illustrate one of these controls. This function allows you to make a list of tasks, assign them to users, set a deadline, and even display the tasks on a timeline or in a calendar. Task lists provide an easy way for users to see and complete tasks. You can take the following steps to work with this control:

1. From your site or subsite, click the Settings icon, then select Add app.
2. On the Site contents page, click the Tasks icon.
3. Give the task a name and then click the Create button (as shown in Figure 2.26).

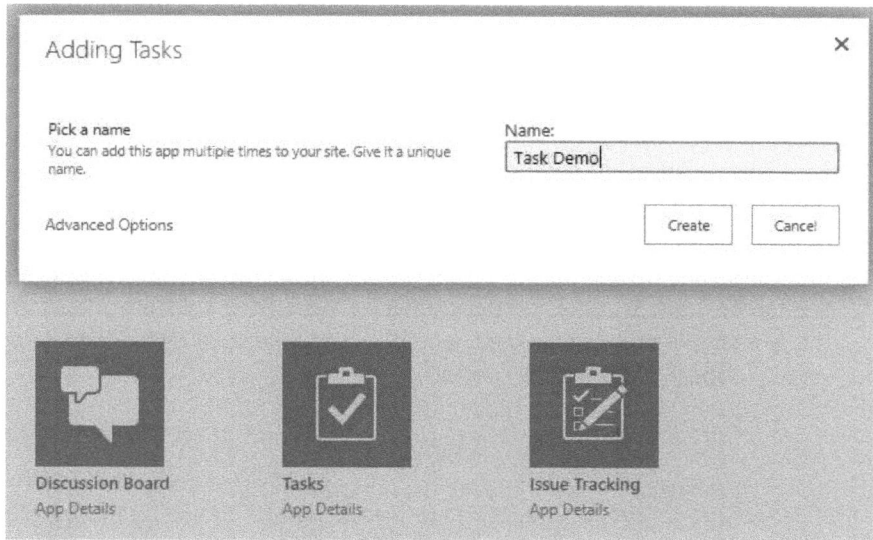

Figure 2.26: Figure Creating a task control

4. Add tasks by clicking the new task link, and add the Task name, Start Date, Due Date, and assign the task to a user.
5. Once you have set up your list of tasks, to add the tasks to the timeline click the ellipses next to each task then click Add To Timeline (Figure 2.27).

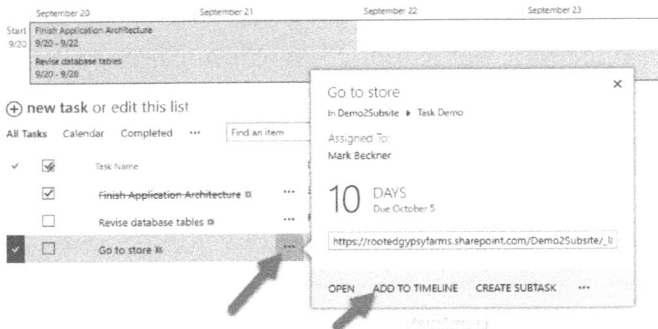

Figure 2.27: Adding tasks to the timeline

6. By default, the task control will be created and available via the Site Contents link in your site. You can click on it and configure it. In Figure 2.28 the task control has two tasks: the first has been completed, the second has a time frame assigned to it. At the top of the screen is a timeline showing when tasks need to be done. You can add dependencies, priorities, and status. In short, this is a simply project management tool that can be used by individuals or small groups to manage their projects.

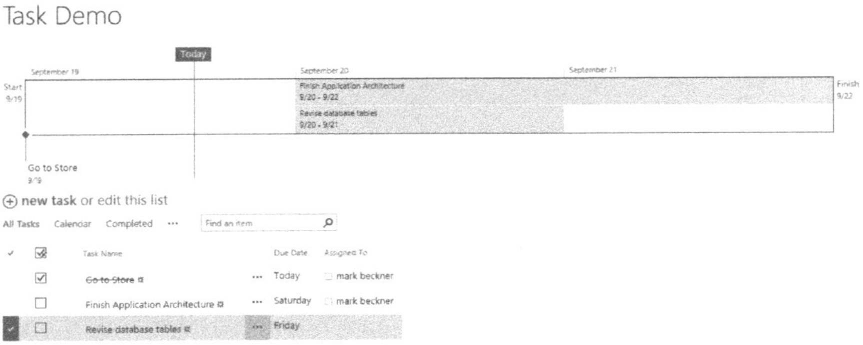

Task Demo

Figure 2.28: The task app

Make sure to explore all the apps that are available—many have been around for years and have extensive functionality behind them. You will likely be able to apply them to your own environment with relative ease.

Summary

Once you've read through this chapter you'll have the tools necessary to build out your own basic SharePoint site and enable standard functionality. More advanced customizations, alterations in the look and feel of your site, backend code solutions, and workflows will be covered in later chapters, however many environments don't utilize those components. If you are simply setting up a document repository where data can be shared with users, or users can collaborate with each other on documents, you should be set to go right now!

Chapter 3
Styling and Visuals

The intent of this chapter is to review each of the main areas within SharePoint that allow for customizing the look, feel, and operation of your sites. Many hours have been spent on finalizing colors and layouts on customer interfacing websites. Thankfully, much of the branding of your SharePoint Online sites can be done with ease. The ability to drop web parts and add functionality is quick and easy.

Know that there are limitations in what you can do with your styling in an Online environment. With a SharePoint on-premise implementation you have access to the underlying style sheets and code files, and (if you have lots of time for development) you can make extensive modifications to the layout and look of SharePoint. However, in the Online version, you don't have access to these files and are thus limited in what you can do in your styling.

Basic Styling

We will dive into styling by reviewing how to apply a visual template to your site. There are several templates that you can apply that will change the overall color scheme of your site and the apps within it. You can access this by clicking the "What's your style?" icon on the home page of your site or by clicking the Settings icon, then clicking the "Change the look" option (see Figure 3.1).

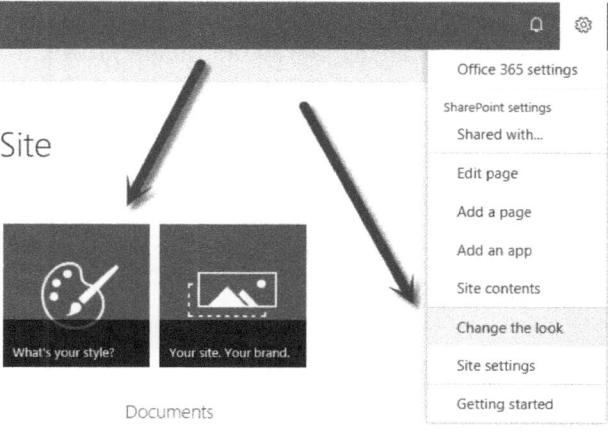

Figure 3.1: Change the look of your site

DOI 10.1515/9781547401253-003

After selecting Change the look of your site, a long list of color schemes and layouts displays. Simply click the one that you want to use and you will be given an option to "Try it out." Click the "Try it out" link and a preview window of your site with the new color scheme will appear. You can decide whether to keep it or try a different option. Several of these options are shown in Figure 3.2.

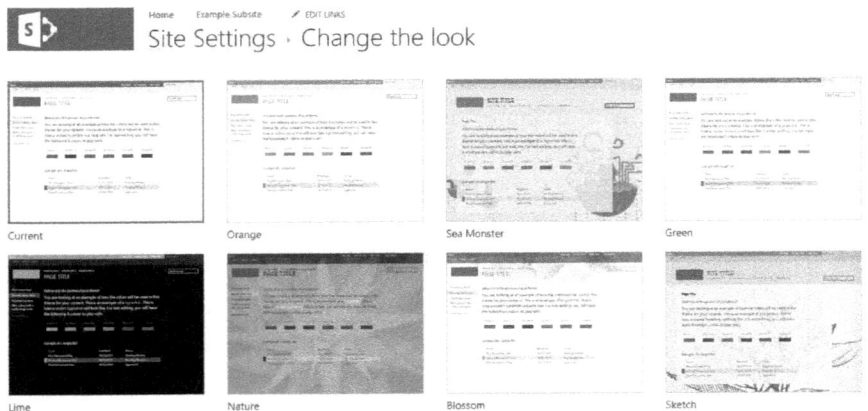

Figure 3.2: Layout options and color schemes

Note that changing the look on your main SharePoint site is slightly different from changing the look and color on a subsite. The steps to open the options for changing the look of your site or subsite are the same but the options are slightly different between the two.

Other actions that can be taken are renaming your site and adding a logo. You can modify the name and logo by clicking the Settings icon, selecting Site Settings, and selecting "Title, description, and logo." This will open a screen where you can make the changes you would like, as shown in Figure 3.3. Your logo will appear in the upper left corner of the screen throughout your site.

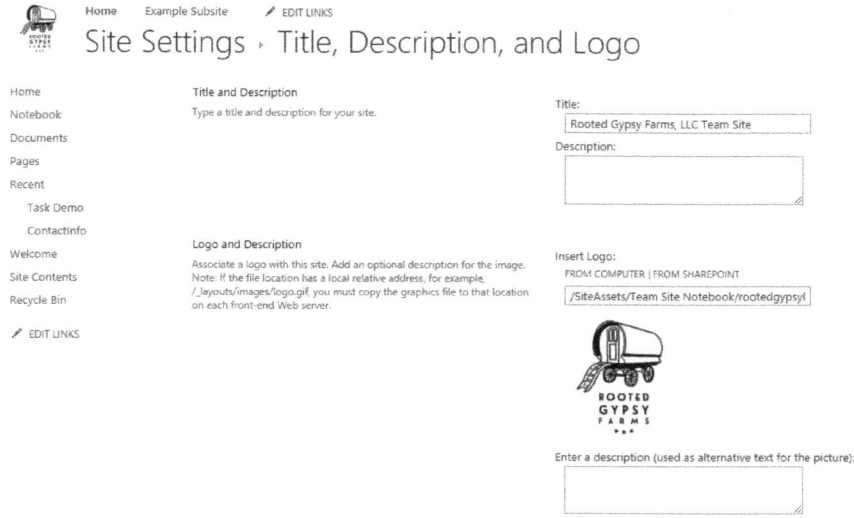

Figure 3.3: Altering the logo and the site name

Creating a Site Based on a Different Template

When you create your site, you have the option to base it on several templates. Let's look at creating a site based on one of these templates, the Communication Site. Start by navigating to the top level of your SharePoint structure, which can be done by clicking on the SharePoint option at the top of any site page or by browsing to the base URL. Once there, click the Create site tab at the top of the screen and select Communication Site (see Figure 3.4). There are several layouts that can be chosen within this site template. The screen shown will give a static preview of what this looks like for standard and mobile devices.

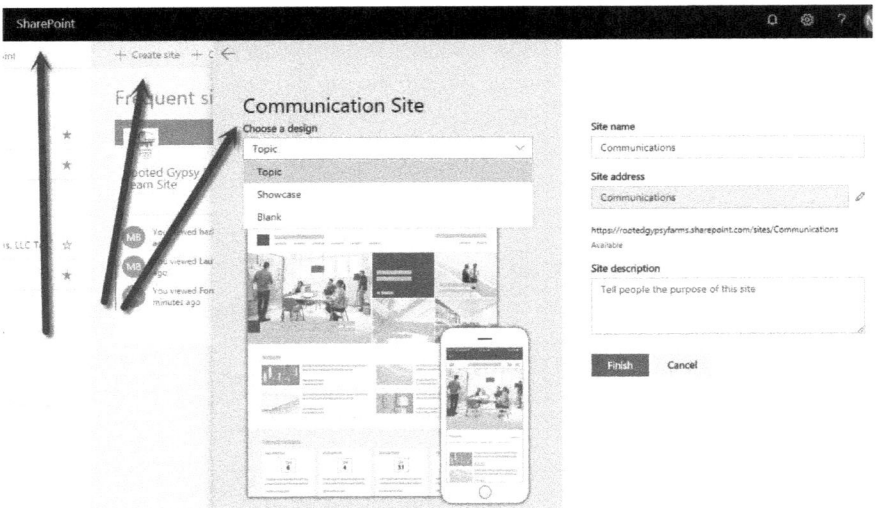

Figure 3.4: Choosing an alternative site template

Enter the Site name (which will automatically complete the Site address) and a brief Site description, then click Finish.

Clicking the Finish button will cause the new site to generate a display. The tiles that appear are actions that users can take to engage with this site. For example, in Figure 3.5 you can see what is called the "Hero web part," which is a web part that consists of multiple functions and areas of configuration. Click the Edit tab for this page to move the various tiles around in this web part. Clicking Edit allows you to edit, add, or delete each functionality on this page.

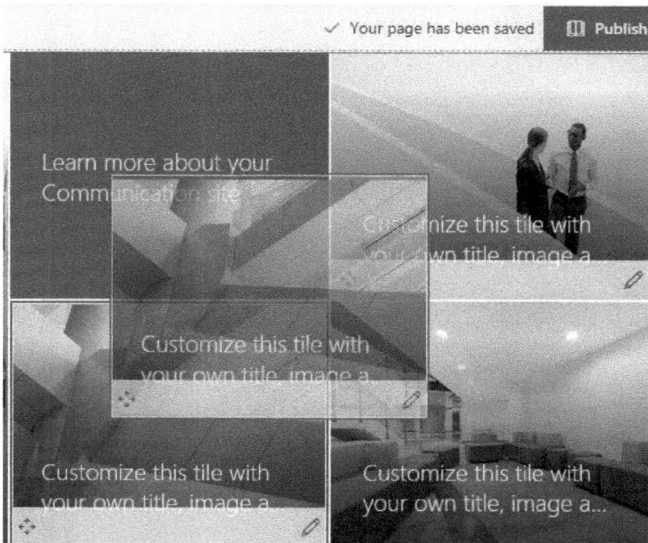

Figure 3.5: Moving the tiles in the default Hero web part on the Communications template

When you edit one of the tiles (refer to Figure 3.6) within the Hero web part, you will be able to change the image and the link that the user will be redirected to when they click it. The idea here is that you would create a series of pages within your site collection, each being a landing page when one of these tiles is clicked. This communications landing page is essentially a dashboard that users would find themselves on when they log into the SharePoint site, allowing them to easily navigate around the system.

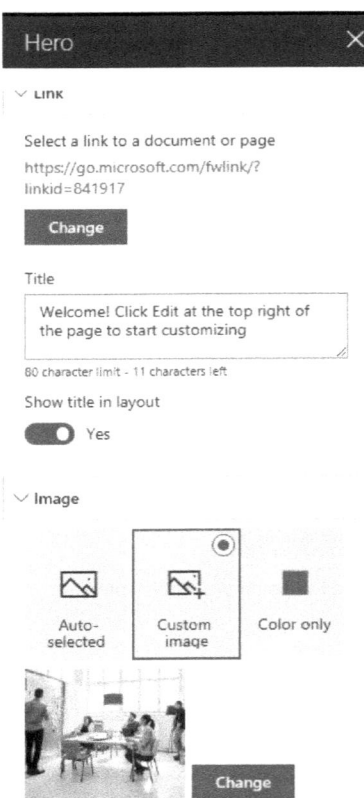

Figure 3.6: Editing a tile in the Hero web part

Navigation

The default navigation that SharePoint provides is acceptable for simple site structures, but if you have a complex site with many components, you will likely want to revise what links are available to click through the site. There are two navigation sections. The upper set of links is called the Top Link Bar, while the left-hand column is called the Quick Launch.

On a main site page, you have two options to alter the links that are on the Top Link Bar. You can click the Top Link Bar option in Site Settings or you can click the Edit Links button at the top of the screen. Figure 3.7 shows a link being dropped in the "Drag and drop link here" option. You can also click the "+ link" option to give a name and add a URL.

Figure 3.7: Adding a link to the Top Link Bar

The Quick Launch bar can be edited as well by clicking the Quick Launch link in Site Settings. This will open the screen shown in Figure 3.8. Here you can add as many links and headings as you want. As you add, remove, and reorder items on this screen, it will update the actual navigation bar on the left in real time. The links that you add can be links to internal SharePoint URLs within your site or they can be external links to other websites.

Home Example Subsite ✏ EDIT LINKS	
Site Settings › Quick Launch ⓘ	
Home	🗎 New Navigation Link	🗎 New Heading	🗎 Change Order
Notebook	
Documents	🗎 Home
Pages	🗎 News
Recent	🗎 Notebook
Task Demo	🗎 Documents
ContactInfo	🗎 Pages
Welcome	🗎 Recent
External Links	🗎 Task Demo
Link to Google	🗎 ContactInfo
Site Contents	🗎 Welcome
Recycle Bin	🗎 External Links
	🗎 Link to Google
✏ EDIT LINKS	🗎 Site Contents

Figure 3.8: Altering the Quick Launch navigation

For sites that have many nested components, such as subsites or document libraries, you may want to enable a dynamic tree view option so that users can quickly get at the information they need. From the Site Settings page, click Navigation Elements. By clicking the Enable Tree View option on this screen, a classic "Windows Explorer" component will be added to the quick launch navigation bar. Figure 3.9 shows what this looks like in action.

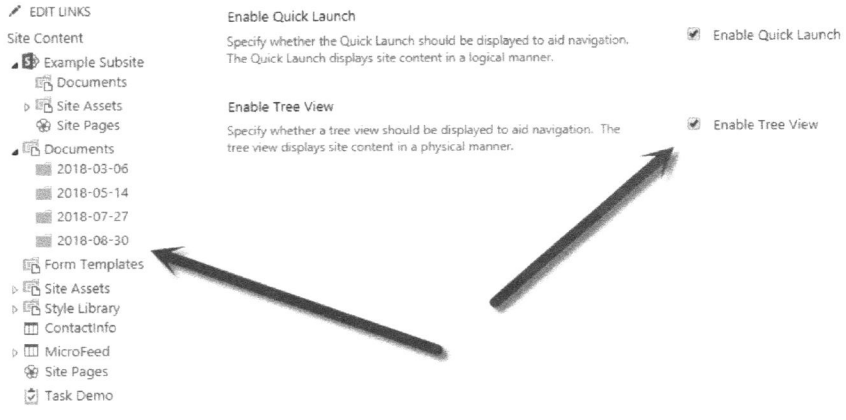

Figure 3.9: Enabling the Tree View for navigation

Modifying Pages

Throughout SharePoint, you will notice an "Edit" tab on virtually every page and component. The ability to customize SharePoint is built into the functionality. Some of these controls offer basic ways to modify functionality and look, as previously outlined in this the chapter. Other areas allow for extensive customization. Altering a page within your site is an example of a component that has extensive built-in options for layout changes. To demonstrate this, click the Edit button in the upper right-hand corner of your site's home page (see Figure 3.10).

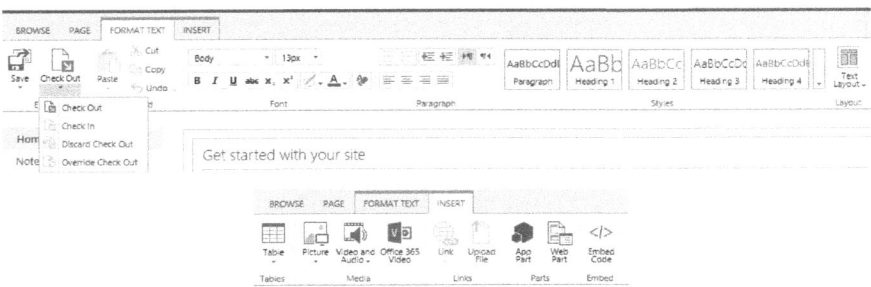

Figure 3.10: Toolbars available when a page is being edited

Clicking the Edit link will open the page in edit mode and provide several options, including the following:

1. Check Out the page for editing. Just like a document, you can collaborate on a page. Check Out the page to ensure it is locked while you are working on it.
2. Add text and style it with standard word processing options (color, size, highlights, etc.).
3. Alter the layout of the page. You can divide your page into a single column, multiple columns, and several other layouts, as shown in Figure 3.11.

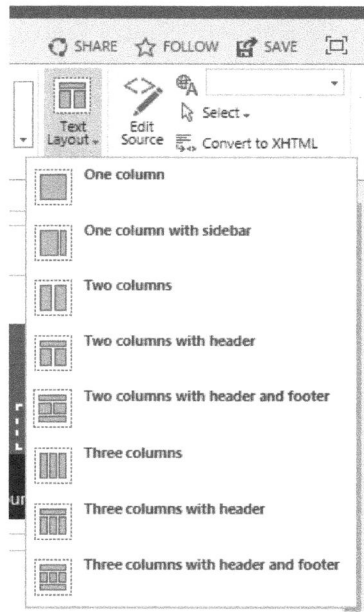

Figure 3.11: Altering the page column layout

4. Alter the HTML of individual controls (click the Edit Source tab to do this). You can click a control within the page layout and customize the HTML as you need. In Figure 3.12, the top HTML is the default provided by SharePoint. The lower section provides a simple modification. The result of the modification is shown in the published page below the code. Altering the HTML gives you some additional control over the look of your site page.

Figure 3.12: Editing the HTML of a control within the page being edited

5. Add images, videos, links, and files by clicking on the respective option on the Insert tab.

6. Add a web part to your screen by clicking on the Web Part icon on the Insert tab. This will let you browse through your site to add a web part. Chapter 4 will show you how to add a custom web part to your page.

7. In addition to all the functionality available in the editing toolbars, you can also drag and drop the controls in the page to alter the layout.

Embedding a Document in a Page

You can embed a document within a page using the Embed code functionality of SharePoint. Embedding a document lets users view the document directly in the page without having to open it in an external page or application. To see an example of this, start by opening a Word document in Word Online. Click the File option on the toolbar and click Share. Select the Embed tab as shown in Figure 3.13.

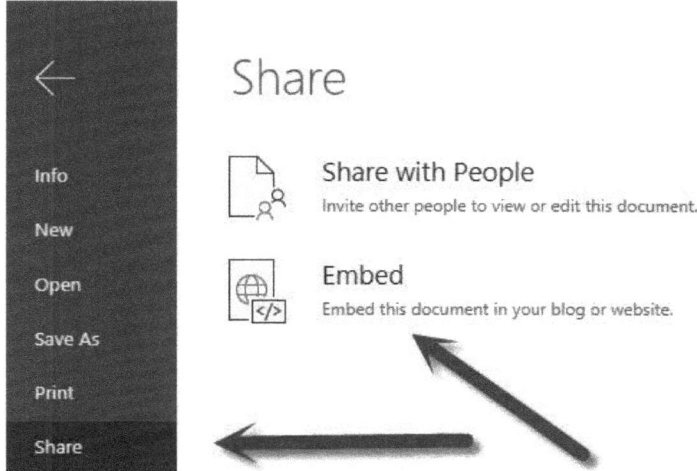

Figure 3.13: The Embed tab in Word Online

In the window that opens, you will see a preview of your document as well as an embedded code segment (see Figure 3.14). You can adjust the height and the width of the embedded document as well as determining what page the document will start on and whether it can be printed. Copy the code from the Embed Code field and return to SharePoint.

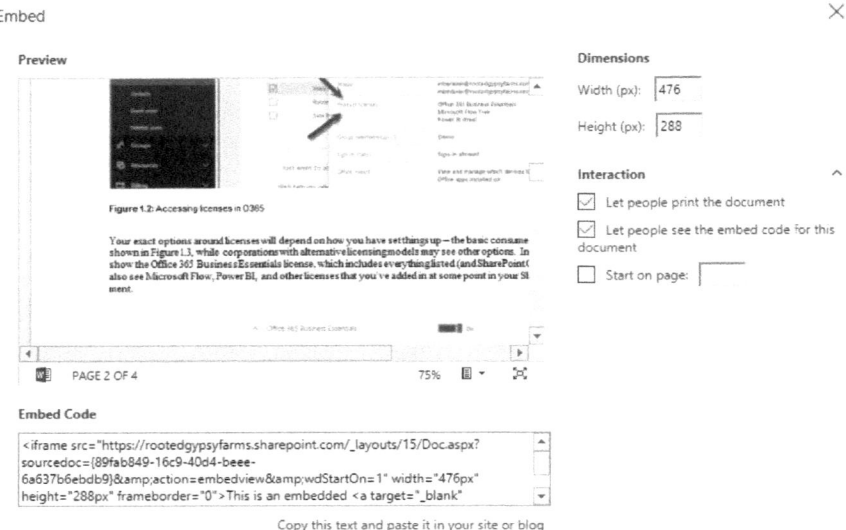

Figure 3.14: The embedded code generated for the document as well as additional settings

Back in SharePoint, we will embed this document directly on the home page by clicking the Edit button in the upper right corner of the site. On the Insert tab, click the Embed Code button and paste the code you copied earlier into this box. Once done, click the Insert button. Figure 3.15 shows this in action.

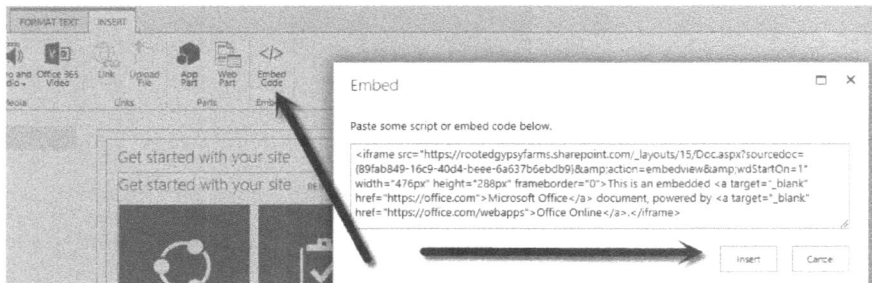

Figure 3.15: Adding the embedded code to the home page

When the home page being edited is saved, the change will be published and the document will be part of the functionality available to users. Figure 3.16 is a screenshot of what the embedded document looks like in the fully published page. Note that there are some options associated with the document, including the ability to zoom in/out, read in full screen mode, and download or print a copy.

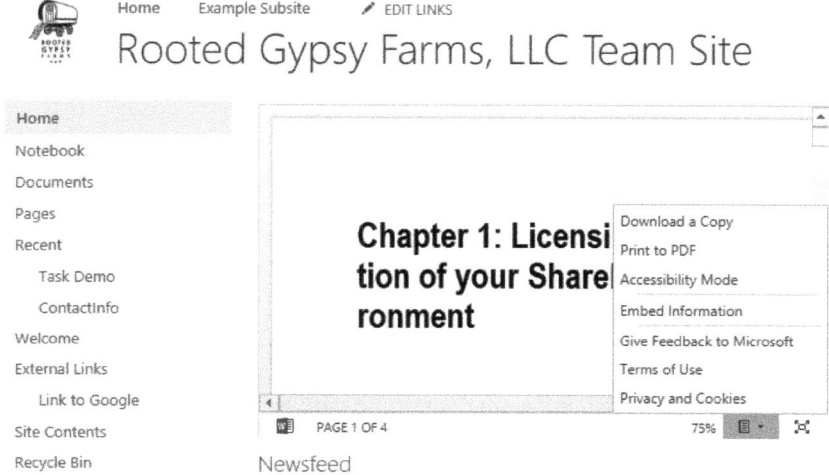

Figure 3.16: Adding the embedded code to the home page

Adding a Chart

The chart control that is available allows you to create a simple bar or pie chart of static information. While of limited value because it cannot be made dynamic, it is quick to use and could be manually updated to display changes over time. To work with this control, edit a page within your site. Click the "+" icon anywhere on the page being edited to display the list of available controls. Click the Quick chart option shown in Figure 3.17.

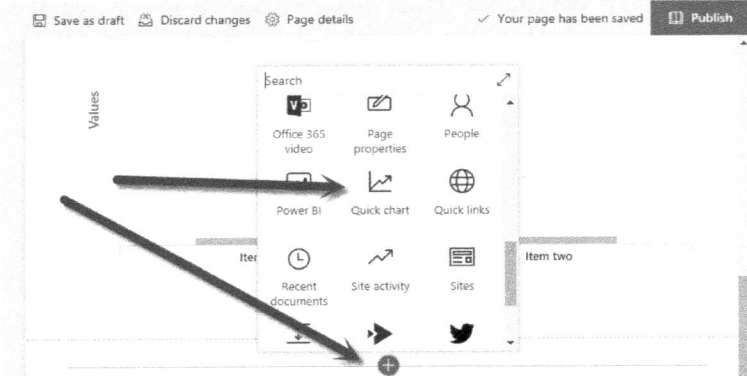

Figure 3.17: The Quick chart control

After clicking the web part icon, you will have several items to configure. Start by naming the chart and then enter the labels and values for the data you want to display. Figure 3.18 provides an example.

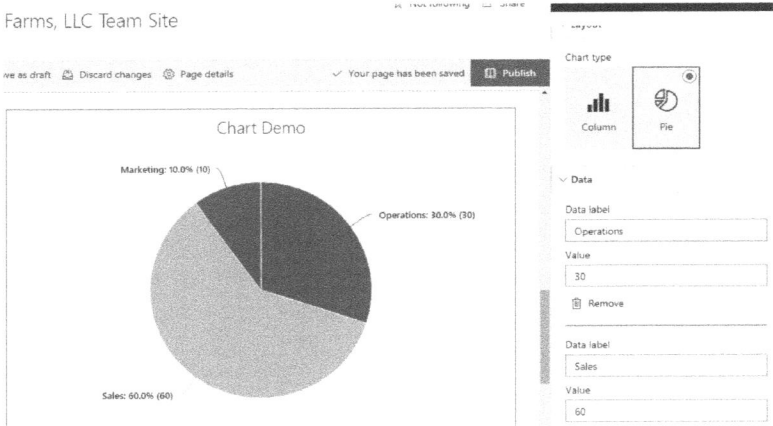

Figure 3.18: Adding data to the static chart control

If you want to display dynamic chart or report content, you have several options.
1. You can use the Power BI control to link to an active report that you have created. You will have to create this report using Power BI (outside of Share-Point). You then take the link to that report and paste it into the Power BI control in SharePoint.

2. Use the Excel Web Access web part. This requires that you create your report in Excel. When you have an Excel report to link to, you can add the Excel Web Access web part to your page. This is available with enterprise licensing only.
3. You can write custom code. There are patterns and examples online for JavaScript-based charts that pull their dynamic data from existing SharePoint lists. You can also custom code your own web part to display information.
4. There are several third-party controls that can be purchased and added into your SharePoint solution.

Using Microsoft Forms for Surveys

The Microsoft Forms component is the final web part that we will look at. This web part allows you to create interactive functionality for your users in the form of surveys, quizzes, and polls. To work with Microsoft Forms, click the "+" icon anywhere on a page that is being edited and select the Microsoft Forms icon. The web part will appear on your screen as shown in Figure 3.19.

Figure 3.19: Microsoft Forms for surveys

Click the New form tab. A window will open and prompt you to name your survey. Once done, you will click the Create button. A new frame will open where you can create questions and answers. Start by adding a new question. The types of question options are shown in Figure 3.20.

Survey Number One

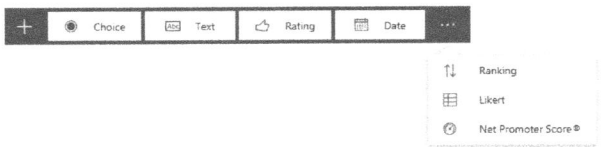

Figure 3.20: Creating a question type

Choice, Text, Rating, Date, and Ranking are obvious, but Likert and New Promoter Score will be new to you. Likert lets you identify a question and then allow for an indicator of how much something is liked, as shown in Figure 3.21.

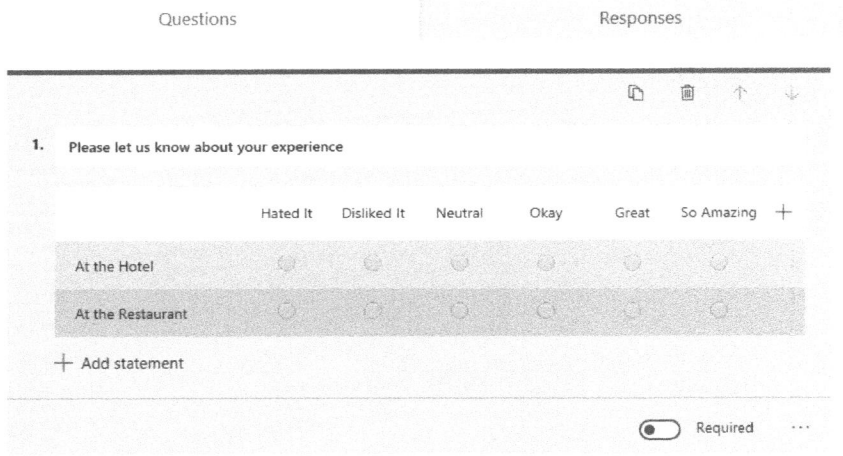

Figure 3.21: Creating a question type

The ability to style your surveys is also available—just click the Theme tab in the upper right-hand corner and choose from one of the options. Figure 3.22 shows what is available by default, but you also can customize themes and create your own.

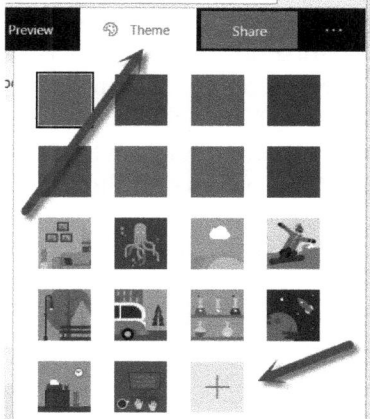

Figure 3.22: Themes available for surveys

For surveys that have nested logic, you can create branching logic by clicking the ellipses in the upper right corner and selecting Branching. The logic here is basic, but it will allow you to skip questions or go to the end of a form, depending on responses.

When the survey development is complete, you can preview it (in computer or mobile views) and then publish it. Publish it by clicking on the Share tab. In this example, we will click the email option and send a link to the survey (see Figure 3.23). The recipient will get the email and be able to click the link.

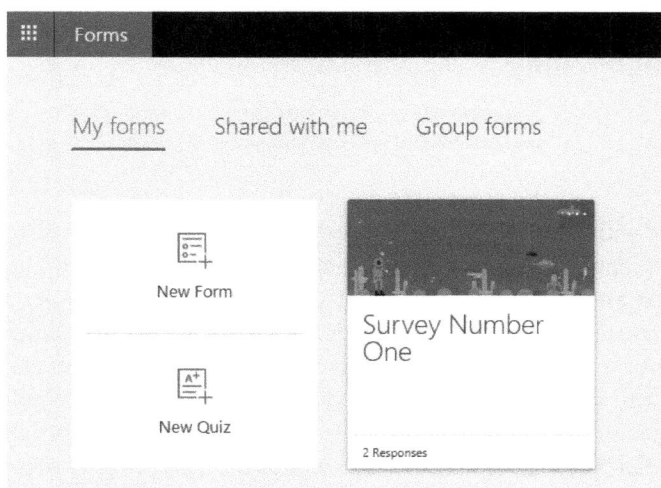

Figure 3.23: A survey form

When the survey has been completed, you will be able to review the responses—but you will need to log into Microsoft Forms to do so. Go to forms.office.com and look at your survey (as shown in Figure 3.24). You will be able to track the results and export to Excel. Microsoft Forms is a cool little tool, and you don't have to use it within SharePoint, as it is its own separate application. But the integration within SharePoint is nice and helps to add interactive visuals to your sites.

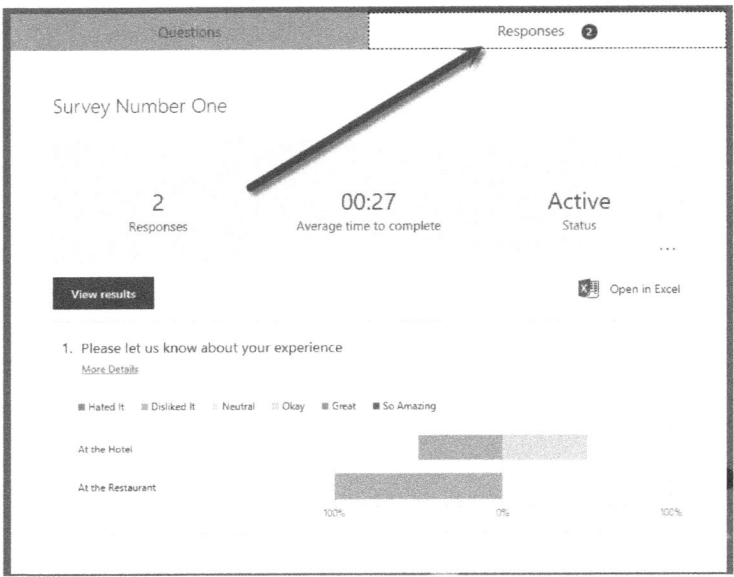

Figure 3.24: Check out the survey results

Summary

You are now familiar with several options to style your SharePoint Online environment. Unlike on-premise editions, there are limitations on what you can do with altering the look and feel of your sites, but the ease with which you can change themes, colors, and layouts makes up for any perceived shortcomings. You can also add several standard web parts and controls to your site. You can bring basic charting and survey functionality into your solution as well. Depending on your licensing with O365, you will have access to different controls but you will come to realize that they are simplified. You will most likely want to build your own web parts, which we will look at in some detail in the next chapter.

Chapter 4
Developing Custom Web Parts

We will now shift and look at a very code-centric piece of SharePoint. There are several things that can be coded on the backend, the most common of which is the custom web part. A web part is code that works behind the scenes and presents a viewable interface to users after it has been placed somewhere on the SharePoint site's layout. Web parts are written in .NET and are compiled in Visual Studio. The compiled code is then deployed to SharePoint and can be added to the site. In this chapter, we will go through the steps required to build and deploy a web part.

A Few Thoughts on Level of Effort

Before we look at the specifics of development, let's first discuss how best to scope the level of effort in building these components. All of us have been asked for estimates to build out components for platforms that we may not be completely familiar with. "How many hours will it take you to build out X and present it in Y?" In this case, there is an easy way to estimate a web part (assuming you are already a .NET developer). The following items will guide you to your estimate:

- If this is your first web part, give yourself about four to eight hours to prepare. This includes getting Visual Studio up-to-date so you can build, figure out how to deploy, and write simple code base (like that shown in this exercise).
- There are client-side web parts, which can be coded that consist of HTML and JavaScript. If you are going to build these, you can use a new command line-based tool called the SharePoint Client-side Solution Generator. While this tool is a poor development alternative to Visual Studio, it does give you options to test and view your web part without having to deploy it to Share-Point first (as opposed to Visual Studio, which requires that you deploy first in order to test). The bane of web part developers in older versions of Share-Point is the fact that testing took a lot of extra steps (due to having to deploy first). Realizing that the solution to this is the SharePoint Client-side Solution Generator can be disappointing, but it is an option. Give yourself about four to eight hours to ramp up on this tool and then make the decision to skip it and build web parts the old-fashioned way—in Visual Studio!
- For the meat of the standard web part—the portion of the code that does work—determine how long it would take you to code it in a .NET windows application. For example, in this chapter we look at calling a web API that

DOI 10.1515/9781547401253-004

returns stock information. It might take an hour or two for you to work through this, test it, and ensure your code is ready to go. In cases where you have complex functionality in your web part, and you are interacting with SharePoint components and building out complex visuals, give yourself substantially more time to test and debug than you usually would. If you think it would take you two hours to code, give yourself four to six hours.

– Deploying your web part and configuring your site to display it only takes a few minutes, so you might want to estimate and hour or so for deployment activities. Chances are good that you will have to deploy multiple times as you test it, recode, and redeploy it.

– You will spend a lot of your time testing your web part. Using the Visual Studio approach to developing (as opposed to the Client-side Solution Generator), you really can't test your web part unless you put your code in a test app. In many cases, you can develop your web part code in a simple Visual Studio Windows application, test it, and then simply move that tested code into the web part framework and deploy it. But, if your web part is heavy on visual functionality, you'll have to deploy it to SharePoint before you can test it.

– A good rule of thumb for web part development would be as follows (you can use these guidelines if you are being asked to estimate on the fly, especially in an Agile project environment).

  o For a simple web part, give yourself four to eight hours.
  o For a web part of medium complexity, give yourself twelve to twenty-four hours.
  o For a complex web part, give yourself forty or more hours.

Developing a Web Part

Let's get into the details of development. In the example that we'll work through, we are going to create a simple stock ticker. We want a user to be able to type in a stock symbol and get the current value of that stock in return. With this, you'll be able to see all the steps required to create, deploy, and run a fully functional web part.

We'll start by getting Visual Studio ready to go. You should use the latest version of Visual Studio for your work. Begin by creating a new project of type SharePoint Add-in, as shown in Figure 4.1. For this example, we'll name it the "StockSymbolApp," so enter this in the Name field.

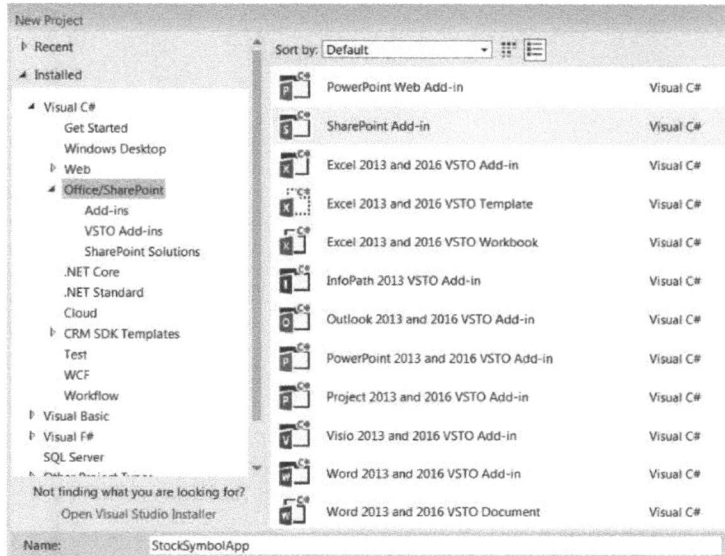

Figure 4.1: A SharePoint Add-in

Next, you'll need to specify the targeted SharePoint site that you'll want to deploy your solution to. There are two options to choose from:

1. Provider-hosted—this is a solution that is hosted outside of SharePoint. For example, it could be on your own web server, within an Azure instance, or anywhere else. For complex functionality, including data that integrates with external systems from SharePoint, you may decide to host your code else-where.

2. SharePoint-hosted—this is by far the most common and follows the classic path of web parts that were available in previous editions. With this option, your code is deployed to and resides within SharePoint itself.

In the case of this example, we will keep things simple and let SharePoint do the work (this is most likely what you will use as well), so select the SharePoint-hosted option (see Figure 4.2).

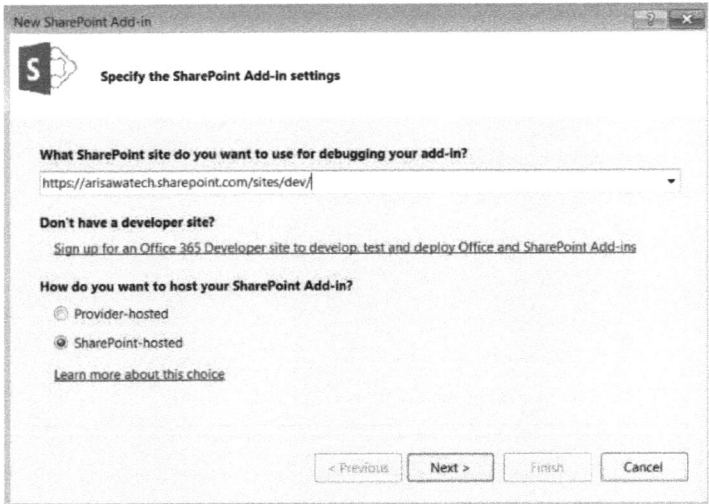

Figure 4.2: Targeting the correct site and host model

After clicking Next, you will get to determine which version of SharePoint you want to deploy to. Of course, and as you can see in Figure 4.3, for this exercise, select SharePoint Online. Once you select this option, click the Finish tab to complete this Add-In wizard process.

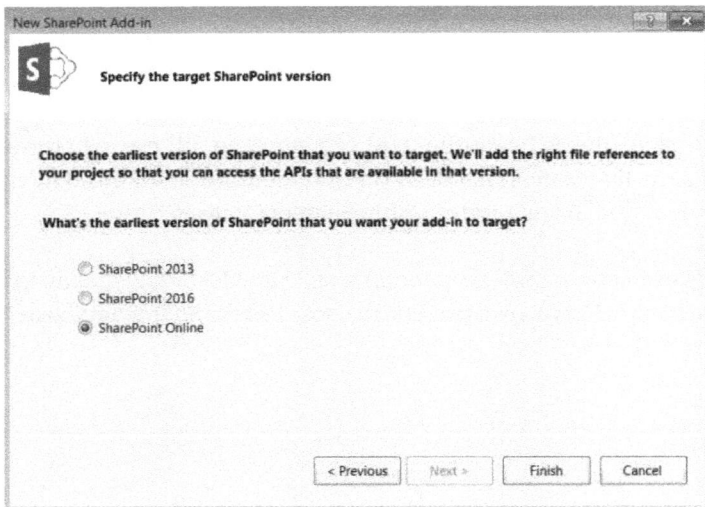

Figure 4.3: Specify the Online version and click Finish

When the wizard completes, your solution will automatically be created for you in Visual Studio. Right click Pages in the StockSymbolApp solution and select Add and then New Item (refer to Figure 4.4). You will be creating a client web part page where you can build out your code that will display within the final web part.

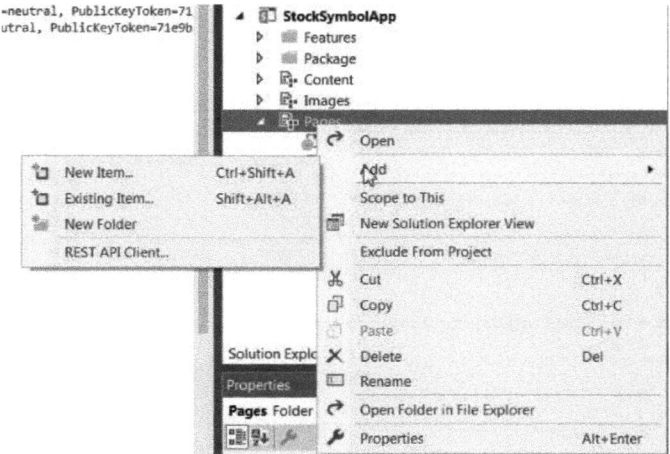

Figure 4.4: Adding a new page to the default solution that was created

In the window that opens, select the Office/SharePoint option on the left and then select the Client Web Part (Host Web) option from the right (see Figure 4.5).

Figure 4.5: Adding the client web part

Immediately after selecting Client Web Part (Host Web), the Create Client Web Part window shown in Figure 4.6 opens. Next, name the page that will be created. We'll keep the StockSymbolApp name and then click the Finish button.

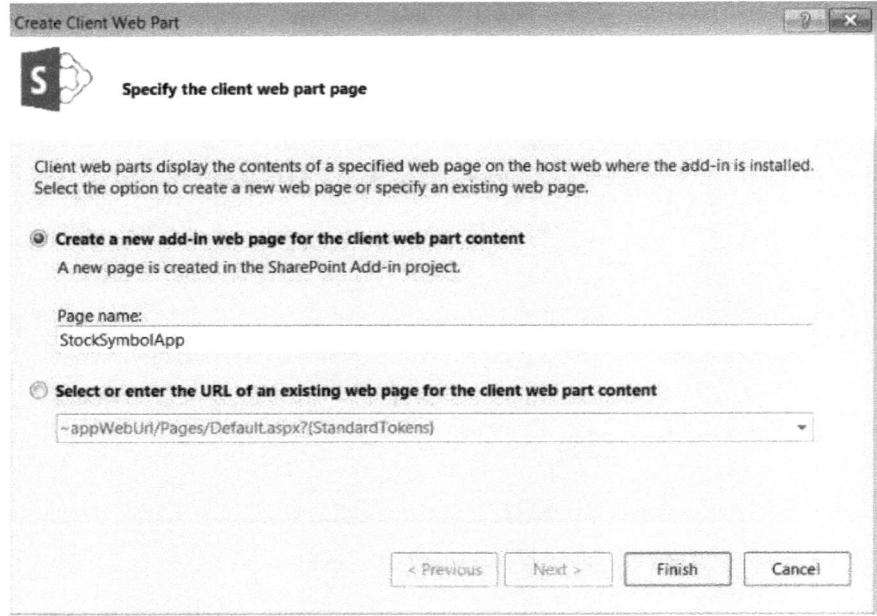

Figure 4.6: Creating the client web part page

With that, you have created your containing page where code can be written (we will refer to this as Page.aspx). Next, you'll need to include the correct references in your solution. This can be done by right clicking your project in Visual Studio and selecting the Manage NuGet Packages option. You're going to add in the jQuery package that is shown in Figure 4.7.

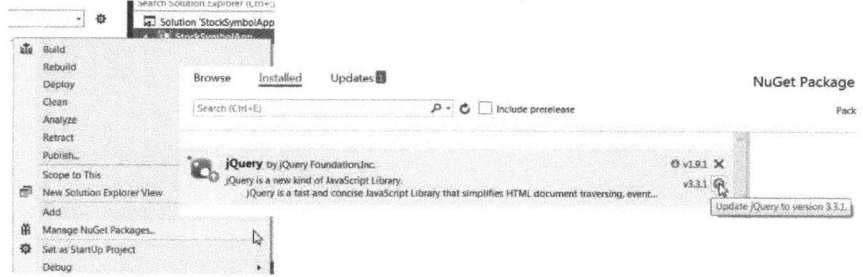

Figure 4.7: Finding the correct NuGet Package can sometimes take some time—make sure and match the version shown!

When you have successfully referenced the jQuery package in NuGet, you'll see the scripts added to your solution. As Figure 4.8 shows, there are several jQuery scripts that will be added.

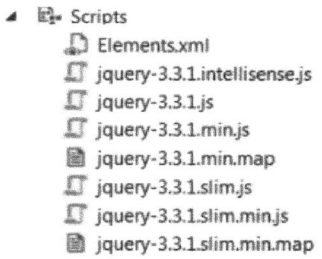

Figure 4.8: The scripts from the package will be automatically added to your project

Web Part Code

You can now begin coding your page! You'll take the following steps, which you can do in whatever order you would like:

1. Create a javascript file to store your custom jQuery code. For this example, we'll call it "App.js."
2. Add a reference to the App.js file and jQuery file to your page.
3. Add the visual content of your web part to the page ASPX file.

Listing 4.1 below shows the code for the App.js file that you need to add. For this example,

Listing 4.1: The App.js code for the example web part

```javascript
$(document).ready(function () {
 $('#getQuote').on('click', function (e) {
  var symbol = $('#tickerSymbol').val();
  var URL = 'https://www.alphavantage.co/query?function=TIME_SERIES_
DAILY&symbol=';
  URL = URL + symbol + '&apikey=OW7YYNETTUQNT9N1';

  $.ajax({
   url: URL,
   success: function (resp) {
   },
   error: function (e) {
    alert('Error: ' + JSON.stringify(e));
    ;
   }
  }).done(function (r) {
   var tbody = $("<tbody />"), tr, th;
   th = $('<tr><th scope="col">Date</th><th scope="col">Open</th>
          <th scope="col">High</th><th scope="col">Low</th><th
scope="col">Close</th>
          <th scope="col">Volume</th></tr>');
   $.each(r["Time Series (Daily)"], function (i, item) {
    tr = $("<tr>" + "<td>" + i + "</td>" + "</tr>");
    $.each(item, function (y, val) {
    tr.append("<td>" + item[y] + "</td>")
    });
    tr.appendTo(tbody);
    th.prependTo(tbody)
   });
   tbody.appendTo("#mainTable");
  });
 });
});
```

This javascript code simply calls an existing REST service, publicly available online, and parses the JSON that is returned. Listing 4.2 below shows an example of the JSON that is returned by this. You can call the service from a browser to see your own results by using the following URL. Just replace the "MSFT" with whatever stock code you would like.

https://www.alphavantage.co/query?function=TIME_SERIES_DAILY&symbol=MSFT&apikey=OW7YYNETTUQNT9N1

Listing 4.2: JSON returned by API call

```
{
  "Meta Data": {
  "1. Information": "Daily Prices (open, high, low, close) and
Volumes",
  "2. Symbol": "MSFT",
  "3. Last Refreshed": "2018-09-20 16:00:01",
  "4. Output Size": "Compact",
  "5. Time Zone": "US/Eastern"
  },
  "Time Series (Daily)": {
   "2018-09-20": {
   "1. open": "112.2800",
   "2. high": "113.8000",
   "3. low": "111.9300",
   "4. close": "113.5700",
   "5. volume": "19472318"
  },
   "2018-09-19": {
   "1. open": "113.0500",
   "2. high": "113.3200",
   "3. low": "111.0350",
   "4. close": "111.7000",
   "5. volume": "21662633"
  },
   "2018-09-18": {
   "1. open": "112.1900",
   "2. high": "113.6950",
   "3. low": "111.7200",
   "4. close": "113.2100",
   "5. volume": "22170934"
  },
   "2018-09-17": {
```

```
  "1. open": "113.6900",
  "2. high": "113.7000",
  "3. low": "111.8600",
  "4. close": "112.1400",
  "5. volume": "20736516"
 }
 }
}
```

When the App.js file has been completed, you can then add it to the script section of your Page.aspx file. You also need to remove the default script references and add a reference to one of the jQuery files that were added when you referenced the NuGet package. The script section of your file should look like that shown in Figure 4.9.

```
<title></title>
<script src="../Scripts/jquery-3.3.1.js"></script>
<script src="../Scripts/App.js"></script>
```

Figure 4.9: The script section of the Page.aspx file needs to refer to the two .js files

The next step is to add the custom code to the body of the page. This code represents the visual aspect of the web part and is what will display once the web part is added to a site within SharePoint. Listing 4.3 shows the code in the Page. aspx file with the revised script content and custom code within the <body> tag. The key pieces of functionality added to this web part are:

1. The text box called "tickerSymbol," where the user can type in the stock symbol they want to get results for. This tickerSymbol value is pulled into the URL in the JavaScript to make it dynamic.
2. The "getQuote" button is clicked to initiate the call to the JavaScript in the App.js file. The getQuote onclick event is triggered when this button is clicked. Javascript will print out the HTML that converts the JSON returned by the service call.

Listing 4.3: The default Page.aspx code with the revised script references

```
<html>
<head>
 <title></title>
 <script src="../Scripts/jquery-3.3.1.js"></script>
```

```
 <script src="../Scripts/App.js"></script>
</head>
<body>
 <nav class="navbar navbar-inverse">
 <div class="container">
  <div class="navbar-header">
   <button type="button" class="navbar-toggle collapsed" data-tog-
gle="collapse" data-target="#navbar" aria-expanded="false" aria-con-
trols="navbar">
    <span class="sr-only">Toggle navigation</span>
    <span class="icon-bar"></span>
    <span class="icon-bar"></span>
    <span class="icon-bar"></span>
   </button>
  </div>
  <div id="navbar" class="collapse navbar-collapse">
   <ul class="nav navbar-nav">
   </ul>
  </div><!--/.nav-collapse -->
 </div>
 </nav>
 <div class="container">
  <div class="searchContainer">
   <h1>Stock Symbol</h1>
   <p class="lead">Enter a Stock Symbol</p>

   <input type="text" id="tickerSymbol" class="form-control" place-
holder="enter as stock ticker symbol (MSFT)"><input id="getQuote"
type="button" value="button" />
  </div>
  <br>
 </div>
 <table id="mainTable" border="1">
  <thead></thead>
 </table>
</body>
</html>
```

With the coding complete, you can now deploy the project to SharePoint for testing. Right-click the project name and select Deploy (see Figure 4.10). This will deploy to the URL that you entered during the Add-in setup earlier in the chapter. If you want to change the URL, just open the properties on the project.

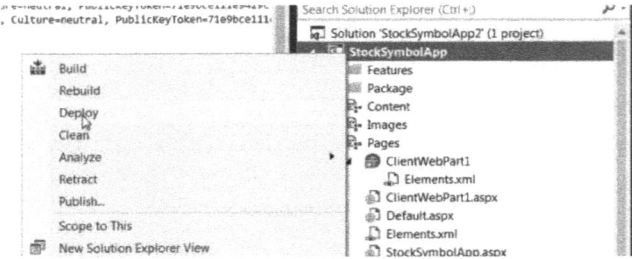

Figure 4.10: Deploying the project to SharePoint

The build process takes places during the deployment, and the status of the build and deploy will display in your build output. A successful build will look like that shown in Figure 4.11.

```
Show output from: Build
------ Build started: Project: StockSymbolApp, Configuration: Debug Any CPU ------
    Successfully created package at: C:\Users\Tarisawa\Documents\Visual Studio 2017\Projects\StockSymbolAp
------ Deploy started: Project: StockSymbolApp, Configuration: Debug Any CPU ------
Active Deployment Configuration: Deploy SharePoint Add-in
    Skipping deployment step because a pre-deployment command is not specified.
    Skipping the uninstall step because the SharePoint Add-in is not installed on the server.
    Install SharePoint Add-in:
    Uploading the SharePoint Add-in...
    Installation is in progress (00:00:00)
    Installation is in progress (00:00:02)
    Installation is in progress (00:00:04)
    Installation is in progress (00:00:06)
    Installation is in progress (00:00:08)
    Installation is in progress (00:00:10)
    Installation is in progress (00:00:12)
    Installation is in progress (00:00:14)
    Installation is in progress (00:00:16)
    Installation is in progress (00:00:18)
    Installation is in progress (00:00:20)
    Installation is in progress (00:00:22)
    Installation is in progress (00:00:24)
    Installation is in progress (00:00:26)
    Installation is in progress (00:00:28)
    Installation is in progress (00:00:30)
    Installation is in progress (00:00:32)
    Installation is in progress (00:00:34)
    Installation is in progress (00:00:36)
    Installation is in progress (00:00:38)
    Installation is in progress (00:00:40)
    Installation is in progress (00:00:42)
    Installation is in progress (00:00:44)
    Add-in was installed at https://arisawatech-b98ad2efca6d25.sharepoint.com/sites/dev/StockSymbolApp2/.
    Successfully installed SharePoint Add-in.
    Skipping deployment step because a post-deployment command is not specified.
========== Build: 1 succeeded or up-to-date, 0 failed, 0 skipped ==========
========== Deploy: 1 succeeded, 0 failed, 0 skipped ==========
```

Figure 4.11: A successful build and deploy of the web part

The deployment having succeeded, you can now go into SharePoint and use the web part. You can add the web part to any existing page by editing the page and clicking the "+" icon or by adding it in from the toolbar. As you can see in Figure 4.12, your web part will display in the list of available items to add to your page. If your Visual Studio deployment was successful, the web part will automatically show in this list.

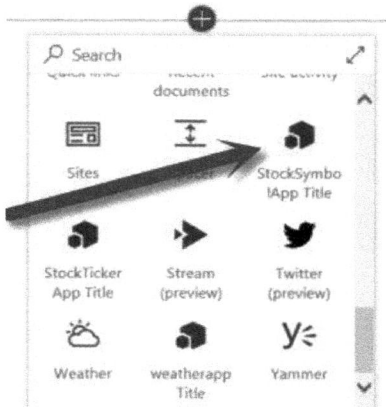

Figure 4.12: The web part is now available in SharePoint to add to a page

After selecting the web part, it will be added to the page. The example code that we built out in this chapter is shown in Figure 4.13. The web part is still in design mode—it must first be published before it will appear on the site for other users. But, you can test it while it'sin design. This is your opportunity to test and debug your code. Keep deploying and testing until you have it working the way you want, then click the Publish tab to share it directly on your site.

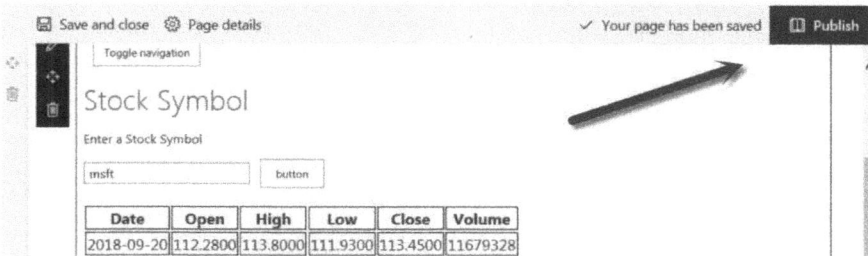

Figure 4.13: Stock Symbol web part

Summary

Focusing on building out a custom web part allows you to see the steps required to deploy .NET developed SharePoint components to your Online environment. There are several other types of customizable objects, but all of them follow a similar pattern. When determining the level of effort and scope of work, focus on the business requirement of the web part itself (what must it do functionally and what would that require to code in any .NET environment) and give yourself plenty of extra time for testing and debugging.

Chapter 5
Workflows

If you think you know about workflows within Microsoft SharePoint because you have built them out in previous versions, you are going to be surprised. While some of the workflow functionality you are familiar with remains, there is an entirely new toolset that has been made available—Microsoft Flow. Flow allows for an entire framework within which business users can configure workflow processes. As a relatively new framework it has some limitations (like any new product), however you'll soon see that it is a great tool, easy to work with, and highly versatile.

Creating a Flow

You can create workflows on almost any entity within SharePoint. The most common place for users to see workflows is at the document level. We'll start at the document level with a simple example of how to spawn a process when an action on a document is taken. To do this, we'll walk through the steps of creating a flow that triggers when a new file is created: based on the user that generated the file, a record will be created in a Dynamics 365 instance. This will allow us to look at Flow templates, logic and conditional steps, and the use of an adapter to create a record in an external system from SharePoint.

Start by clicking on the context menu next to a document in your document library. Select Flow and then Create a flow (as shown in Figure 5.1).

DOI 10.1515/9781547401253-005

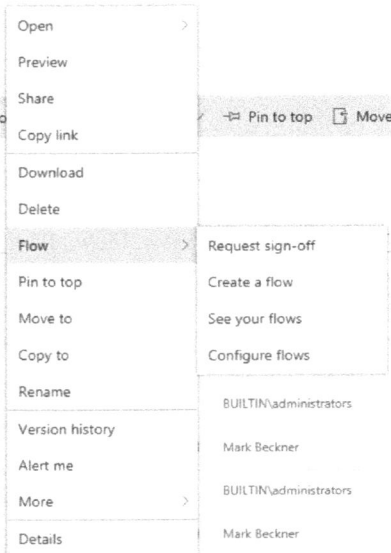

Figure 5.1: Creating a flow on a document

In the window that opens, you'll be able to select from numerous flow templates. It'll take some time to search through the available options since there are so many templates available. There are many flows ready to use such as requesting approval on documents to getting signatures, to posting messages or sending emails when changes occur. Figure 5.2 shows several available flows; additional templates can be added.

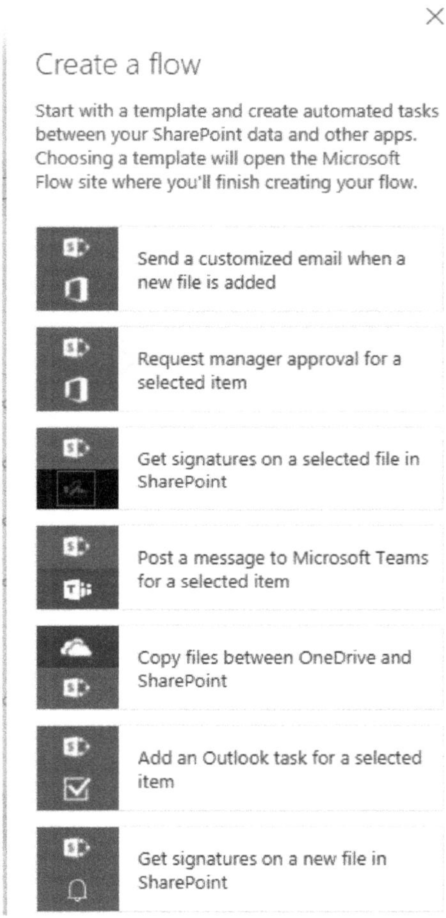

Figure 5.2: Flow templates

For illustration, we will select "When a new file is added in SharePoint, complete a custom action" (see Figure 5.3). When this option is selected, the flow template overview opens in a separate window. You'll now be working within Microsoft Flow, which is a separate application from SharePoint. The splash screen states what the workflow will do. Click the Continue button to move to the next step.

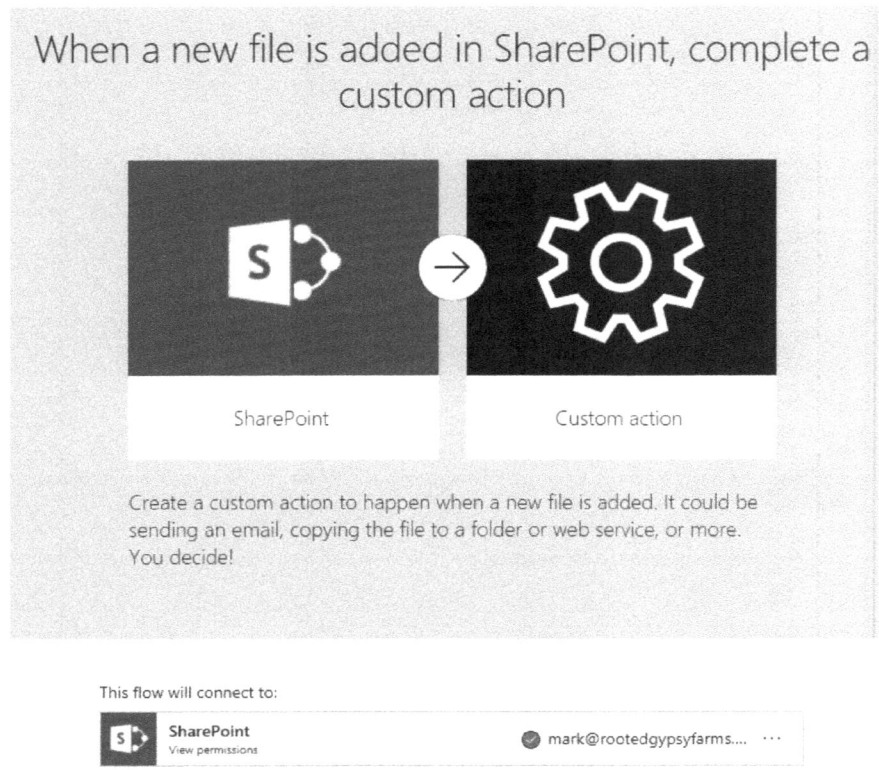

Figure 5.3: Creating a flow based on a custom action template

The development window contains a lot of functionality. Figure 5.4 shows the context menu on the first flow step. To start, click the ellipses at the top of the step, select Add Comment, and enter a comment. Next, in the Folder field, select /Shared Documents. As you can see in Figure 5.4 below, a comment has been added and the /Shared Documents folder, where the flow will occur, has been indicated.

The next step is to add an action. Click + New step, then Add a Condition. The New step option allows you to add an action, add a condition, or add one of several other options. For this example we'll add a condition to the flow.

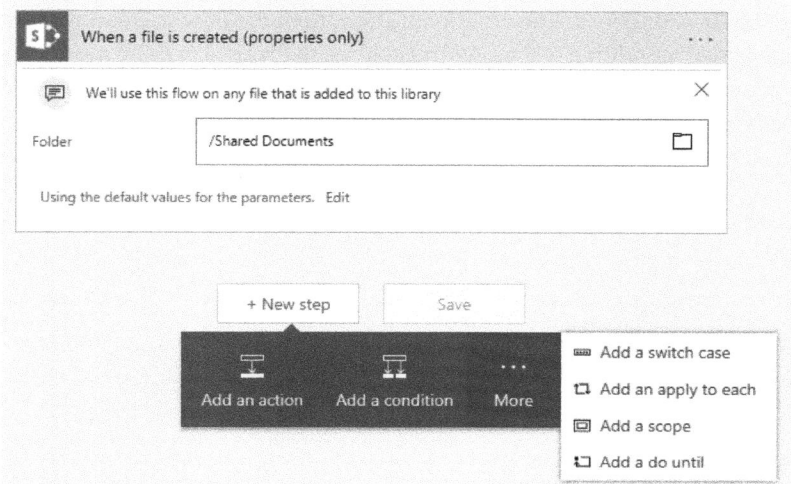

Figure 5.4: The design surface

Clicking the "Add a condition" option in the menu displays the condition parameters and the "If yes," and "If no boxes." We'll configure this case statement to have two settings—if the file has been modified, take one route, if not, take another route. In the Switch box at the top of the screen, click in the box and select the Modified By option. We'll trigger this based on the name of the file that was created. Figure 5.5 shows the rule for this.

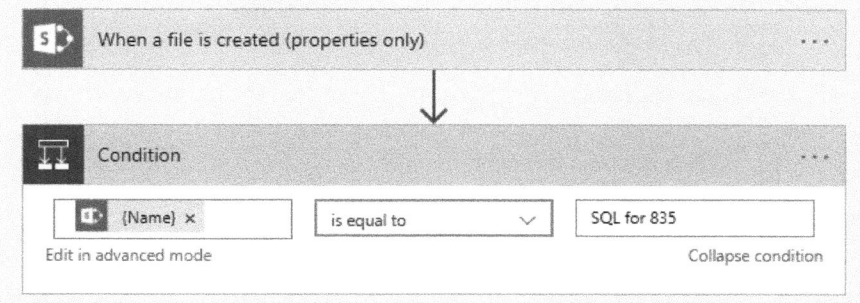

Figure 5.5: The condition

When you have added a condition, two paths will be created. The "true" condition is on the left ("If yes") and allows for configuration. The "false" path ("If no") is on the right and does nothing—the business process just moves on to whatever is next in the flow. If there are no additional steps, then the flow will end without error if the "false" condition is met. As you can see in Figure 5.6, there are a huge number of actions that can be taken if the condition is true (more than 350 when this screenshot was taken!). In the "If yes" condition box, click Choose an action to see this list of options and to make our next selection.

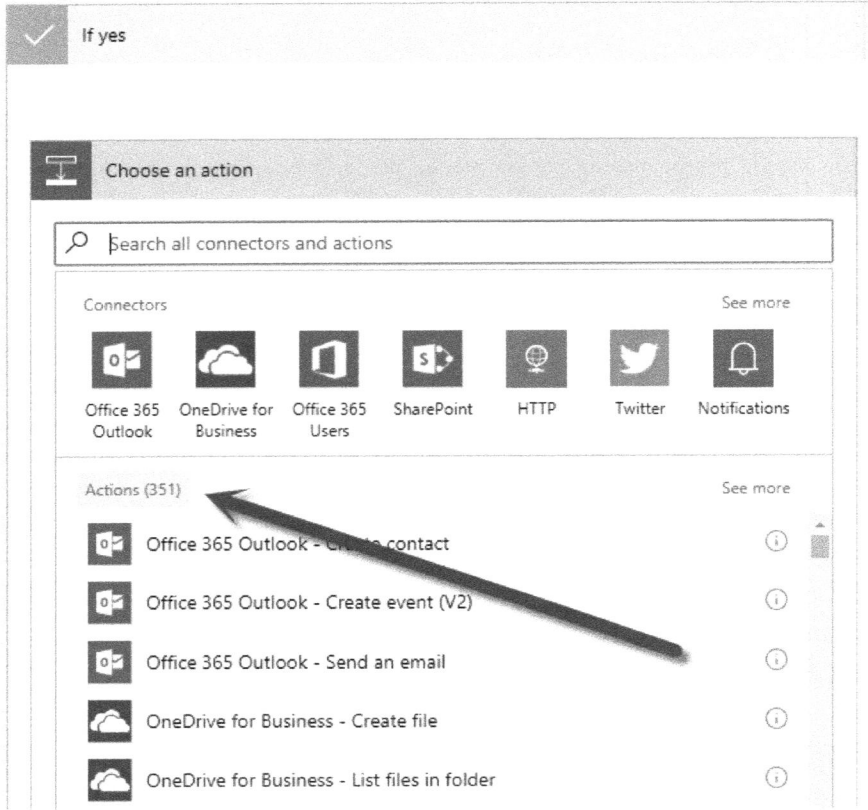

Figure 5.6: Connectors available when the flow condition is true

Flow allows you to integrate with systems across the Microsoft stack, such as Excel, Azure, SQL Server, Dynamics, etc. as well as several third-party tools. The connectors are impressive. For example, if you want to create a record in Microsoft Dynamics 365, select the adapter from the list and configure the connection.

For this example, select "Dynamics 365—Create a new record." You may need to alter the user you are connecting with by clicking on the context menu next to the Create a new record action and click Add new connection (see Figure 5.7). If you do this, you'll have to delete the connector and add it back in so that it logs in with the new user.

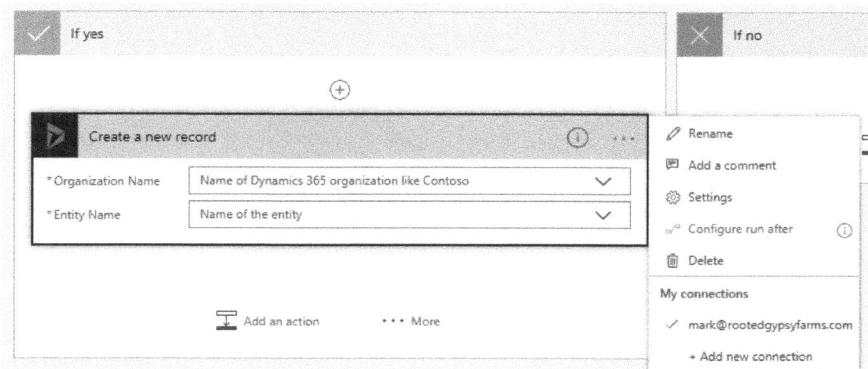

Figure 5.7: Building condition logic in the flow

When you select the target organization and entity name, the list of fields requiring information displays. These values can be static, dynamic values from within SharePoint, or based on code expressions that you develop. In Figure 5.8 the Entity Name field in the CRM Contact entity is being set to the Modified By name of the user that just modified the file.

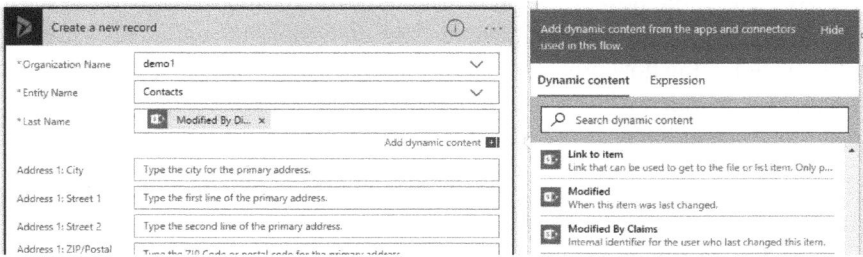

Figure 5.8: Using the Dynamics 365 connector

Flow has a wide variety of functions available for setting values through code expressions. For example, if we wanted to set the Description field on the Dynamics Contact to the name of the person that just modified the file in SharePoint and add additional text to it, we could use the concatenate method in the string functions available in the expression list. Figure 5.9 shows this method being populated.

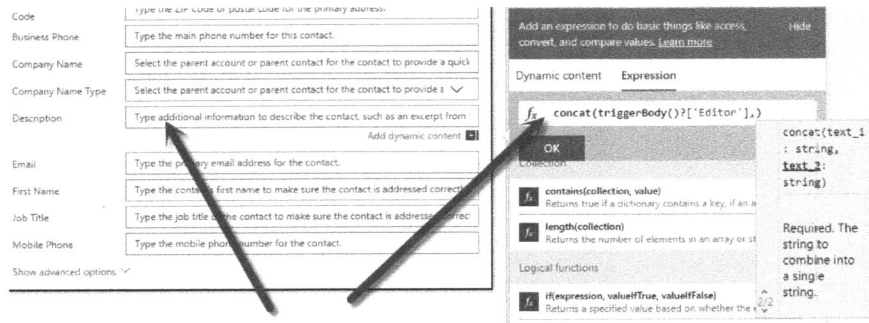

Figure 5.9: Building a custom expression to populate a field dynamically

Testing the Flow

You can continue to add steps and logic to your flow. When you are done, click the Save button, click the Test button, then select "I'll perform the trigger action." This will allow you to manually trigger the first test. You'll now be able to debug the flow you just created. To cause the flow to trigger, a document must be created in SharePoint to match the first condition of the flow we just created. When a file is uploaded in SharePoint, and it matches the naming condition on the user who created the file, the flow will trigger. You can then go into the flow history and see the inputs for each step and whether the step was successful. For example, the first step of the flow process is shown in Figure 5.10. This shows all the input values, one of which is the name of the file that matches the condition required to kick off the workflow.

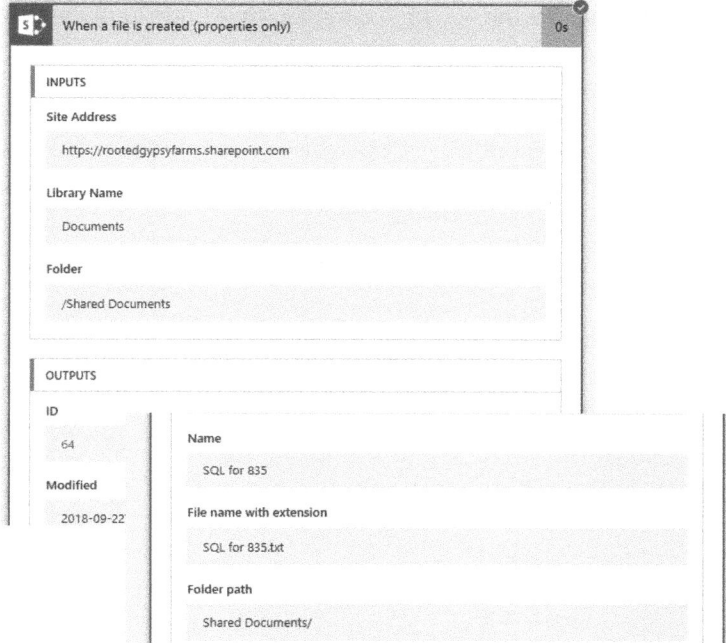

Figure 5.10: The properties on the file are available on the first step of the flow process

The other two steps show that they were successfully executed (see Figure 5.11).

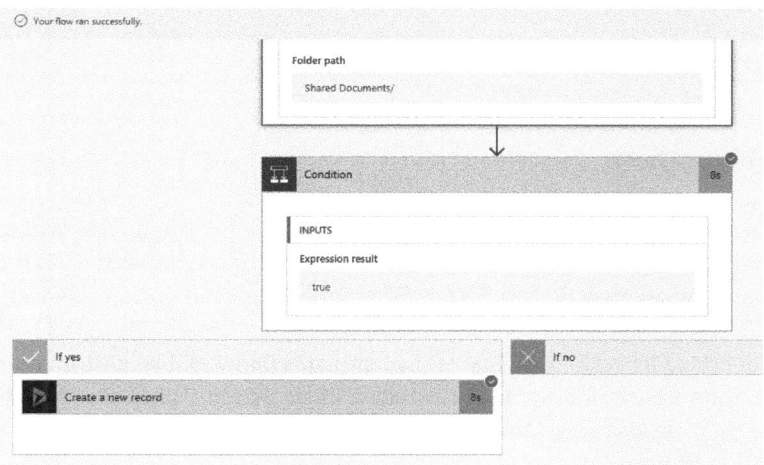

Figure 5.11: Success!

If unsuccessful, you would have the option to retest multiple times until the flow worked as needed. You can choose to work with the same data repeatedly, which speeds up your debugging process. To do this, click the Test button again and select "Using data from previous runs" (if you've tested before, this option will be available). You can then select which test run to use again (see Figure 5.12). By doing this, you don't have to retrigger the action from SharePoint and can use the same data until the results you desire are attained.

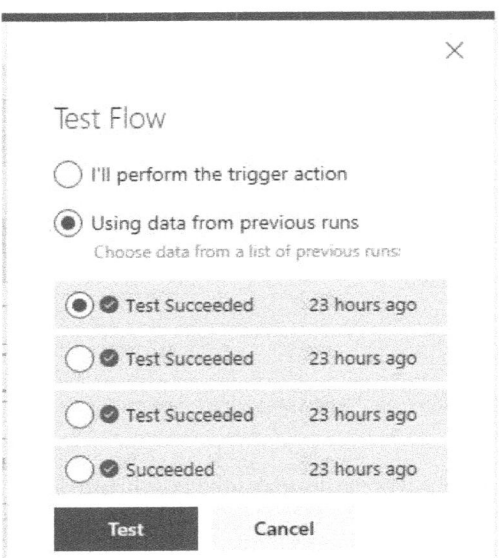

Figure 5.12: Reusing test data that has been previously submitted

Approval Workflow

There are a wide variety of workflow templates available for you to use. Within the Flow website, click the Templates tab and then select the subtab you are interested in. You can see that there are literally hundreds of available templates to choose from. You can create a new one and submit it to Microsoft Flow as a new template for others to work from. One of the templates that you'll want to explore is the Approval Flow, which is one of the oldest ideas within SharePoint. This is the process that lets users collaborate on a document and get signature approvals on it at different stages.

Approvals are an integral part of SharePoint (and now other Microsoft applications) that Flow has an entire section dedicated to it. To access, click on the Approvals tab at the top of the Flow window. In the upper right corner of the window, you will see a button that allows you to create an approval flow. For this discussion we'll look at the "Approve a document using SharePoint Content Approval" template, shown in Figure 5.13.

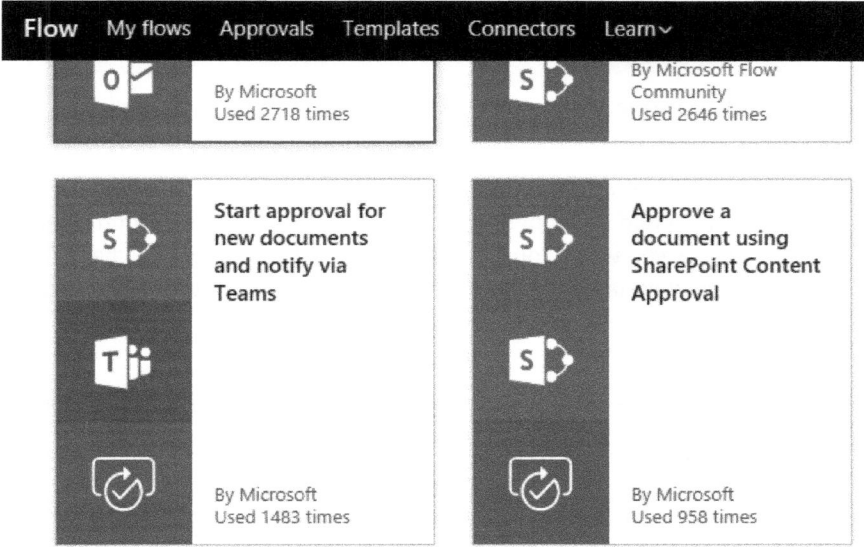

Figure 5.13: An approval template

After selecting the template and clicking Continue, you'll see that the template that opens before you, which is ready for your configuration, is very involved. You can create new steps or modify the existing ones. The default steps that need to be configured are as follows:

1. When a file is created in SharePoint: here you fill in the details about what site, what library, and what folder will be monitored. Figure 5.14 shows these properties configured to trigger on any document created within the main documents folder within the root site.

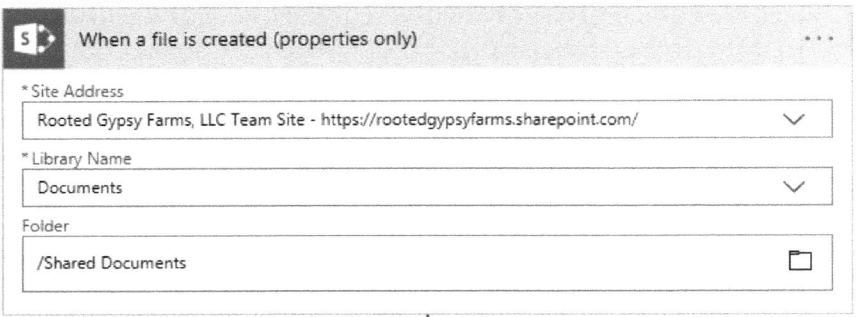

Figure 5.14: Setting the site, library, and folder to monitor

2. Get file metadata: this lets you determine what properties from the file that was created should be brought into this workflow. You can click on as many of the fields as you want. You can see in Figure 5.15 that there are many fields within the metadata of the file, including timestamps, author, file size, file type, etc.

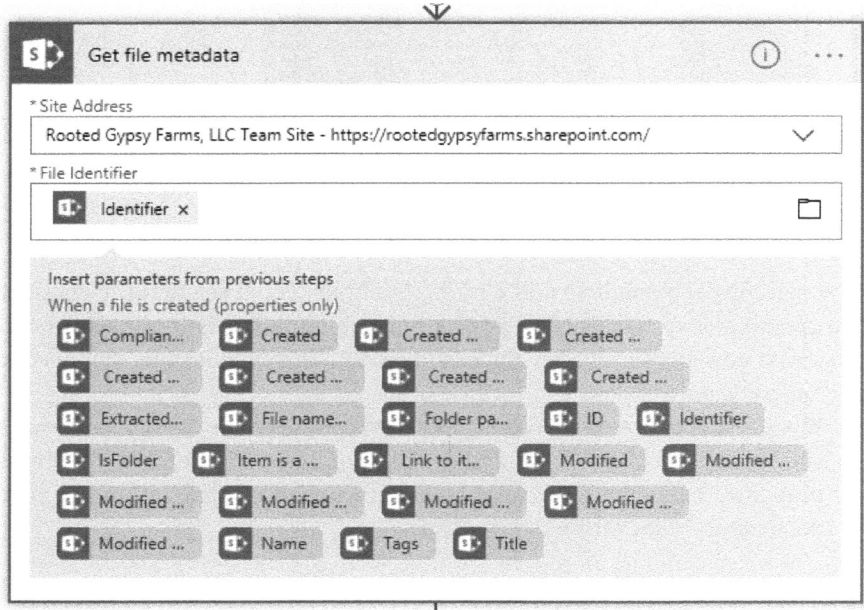

Figure 5.15: All the properties available on a file that can be included in the flow

3. Start an approval: this allows you to define who the document will be assigned to first for approval once it has been checked in, along with what information they will see about the document in the notification they receive. Add one or more emails addressed in the Assigned to field. Note that not all users of the system can be assigned to this depending on their licensing and access permissions.

4. Set the condition: if the response is approved, then set the status to Approved, otherwise set it to Rejected. This logic will be something you will likely want to revise. For example, if the document is approved, you may want to route it to another person for signature or further steps. The template can be altered to your needs. Templates are starting points, not finalized processes. As you can see in Figure 5.16, there are built-in options to start a new approval process directly within your template.

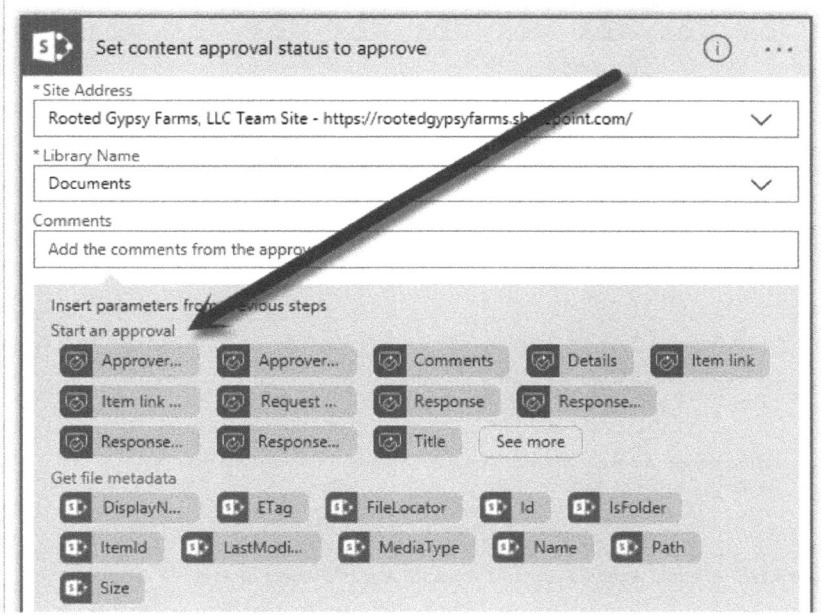

Figure 5.16: You can start a new approval process if needed

An approval workflow can take some work before you have it ready to use, but once you've finished and tested it, you'll see that Flow supports the approval process with easy to access functionality. Click Save to finalize the workflow. To test the flow just created, click the Test icon in the upper right corner of the Flow window.

In our example, if an approval process was just triggered on the creation of a new list item, a user would be notified via email that they need to review a submission. The email that arrives would have an Approve and a Reject button in the email, along with a link to the data to review (see Figure 5.17). The email allows the user to enter a reason as to the details of the approval or rejection. When complete, the recipient of the email clicks the "Submit" button within the email body.

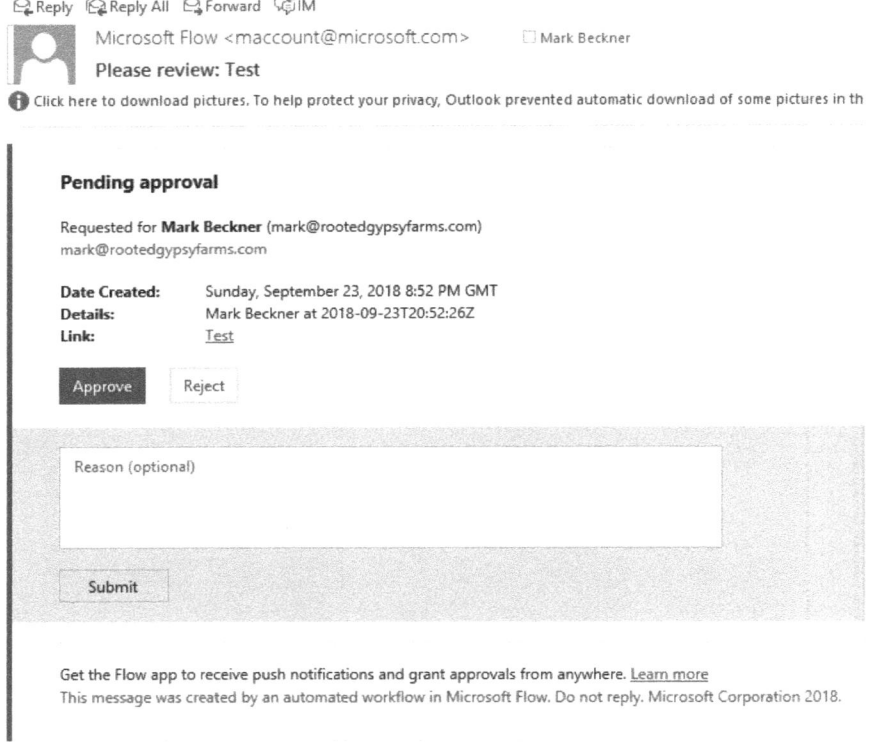

Figure 5.17: An email received contains the Approval and Rejection tabs

Back in Flow, by clicking on the Approve tab, you can see what approvals have been sent and what has been received. Figure 5.18 shows an approval that has been sent and is still awaiting a response as well as a request that has been received and can be approved, rejected, or reassigned. Additional management of flows can be done from this tool as well, as outlined in the next section.

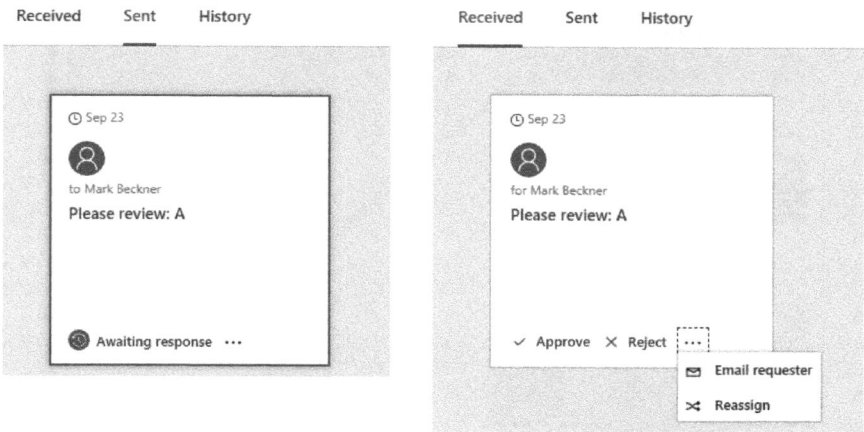

Figure 5.18: Monitoring approval status within Flow

Managing Flows

All management of workflows occurs in Microsoft Flow. You can click on workflow options in SharePoint, but all the actions lead you back to the Flow interface. If you go into Site Settings on your site and click on the workflow settings tab, you'll see a screen where legacy workflows can be monitored. You'd think that this might be an area where workflows could be created or managed, but you'll find that all workflow functionality has been moved to Microsoft Flow. If you have migrated from an on-premise environment, or older online instance, you may see some of your legacy workflows here. If you are in a fresh instance of SharePoint Online, there isn't anything you can do here. To monitor your flows, click on an individual flow's context menu and select See analytics (refer to Figure 5.19).

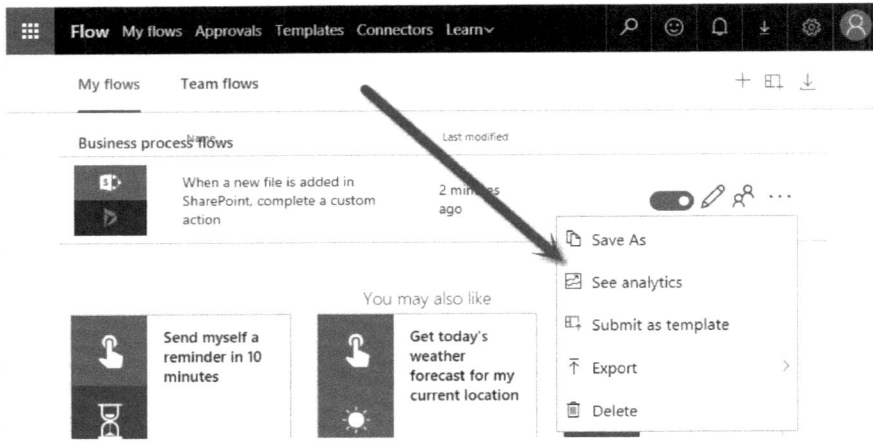

Figure 5.19: Accessing analytics will require a paid license

Unless you have already signed up for a license, you'll get a screen requesting you to sign up for a free trial. If you do sign up, you'll be able to see reports about the usage of your workflow, like those shown in Figure 5.20.

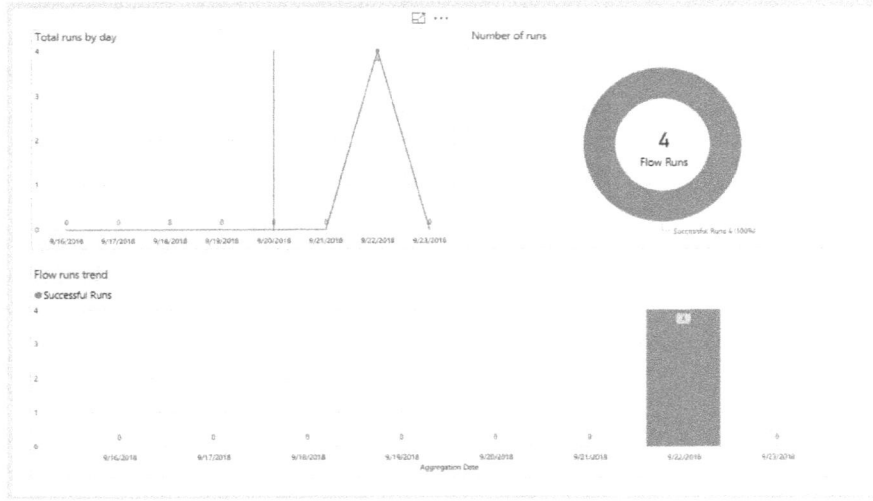

Figure 5.20: An example of analytics on one of the flows

You will receive a notification on your Flow page that indicates processes that have failed (see Figure 5.21).

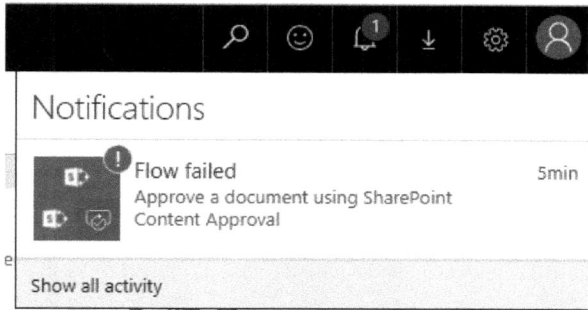

Figure 5.21: A notification that something has failed

You can also see all activity and history of workflows from this area. If you click on the error, you'll be able to see the details behind the failure, and you can work with that failed data and even cancel or resubmit it (see Figure 5.22).

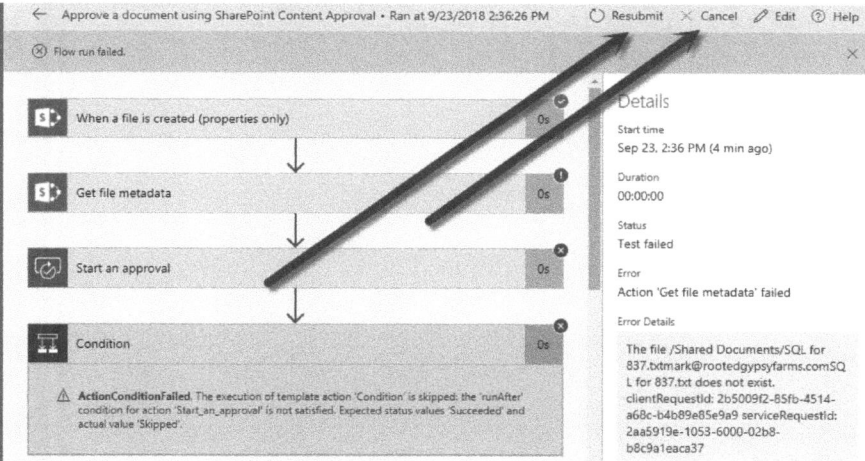

Figure 5.22: Resubmitting or cancelling a workflow

Summary

As you have seen, Microsoft Flow is a powerful tool that is easy to use and can be configured to handle complex workflows. These workflows include standard notifications (such as email and texts) as well as integrations with several end systems (we looked at a simple case with Dynamics 365 in this chapter). The old workflows that used to come standard with SharePoint have all been migrated to Flow, so if you have any workflow requirements, you'll need to get used to this new interface. There are very few limitations with Flow, and there are constantly new templates being uploaded and made available for your use.

Index

.NET 61, 74

A

Access requests and invitations link 7
Accessing analytics 90
Accessing licenses in O365, 2
Active users 2, 7
Active users list 7–8
Active sites 10–11
Adapter 75, 80
Admin centers 8, 21
Admin portal 4, 8–9
Administration 1–2, 4, 6–8, 10–12, 14, 16,
    18, 20
– comprehensive permission 36
Administrators 9, 15
Advanced permissions settings 4–5, 36
Advanced SharePoint development 26
Alert me 31
Alerts 31, 33
Analytics 89–90
App.js file 67, 70
Application 12–13, 52, 60, 77
Approval 76, 85, 87–88
Approval flow 84–85
Approval process 87–88
– new 87
Approval workflow 84–85, 87
Apps 3, 5, 24–26, 29, 35, 38–40, 43
– list of 25, 29
– task 38, 40
Audit settings 17–18
Auditing 17–18
Azure 8, 80

B

Basic document collaboration 34
Border 25, 71
Browse 13, 23, 27, 29, 38, 52
Button 17, 25, 29, 54, 57, 70–71, 77, 82, 85

C

Calendars 38–39
Chart 55–56

Class 71
Classic admin center 10
Classic SharePoint admin center 12
Click finish 46, 64
Client web part 65
– selecting 66
Client web part page 65–66
Client-side web parts 61
Code 51, 53–54, 61–63, 65–67, 70, 73–74
– custom 57, 70
– embedded 54–55
– JavaScript 68
– tested 62
Code expressions 81
Code files 43
Color schemes 43–44
Colors 43–44, 51, 60
Columns 26–28
Communication site 45
Complex web part 62
Components 21, 29, 35, 41, 48, 50, 61
Configuration 31, 33, 46, 79, 85
Configure 12, 33, 40, 56, 79–80
Connectors 80–81
Container 21, 29, 71
Content 6, 8, 12, 14–15, 18, 21–22, 25,
    29–30, 34–35
– controlled 29
– sharing document 23
Content modifications report 18
Context menu 32–35, 37, 75, 78, 80
– flow's 89
Controls 1, 22, 24–25, 38–39, 50–52, 55, 60
– task 39–40
Copy 53, 55
Core SharePoint online functionality 21–22,
    24, 26, 28, 30, 32, 34, 36, 38
Create client web part 66
Customize 24, 51

D

Data, migrated 15
Data migration 1–2, 4, 6, 8, 10, 12–14, 16,
    18, 20

DOI 10.1515/9781547401185-006

Debug 62, 73, 82
Delete a user 8
Deploy 61–64, 71–72, 74
Deployment 72–73
Developing custom web parts 61–62, 64, 66, 68, 70, 72, 74
Dialogue box 33, 37
Directory, default Documents 30
Display 39, 46, 55–56, 62, 65, 70, 72–73
Display information 57
Div class 71
Document center 23
Document collaboration 34
Document libraries 4, 14, 16–17, 21, 30–31, 33, 35, 49, 75
Document repository 41
Documents 16–17, 24, 26, 30–35, 37–38, 51–55, 75–76, 84–85, 87
Documents folder 85
Documents link 30
Documents tab 24
Download 12–13, 55
Drag and drop 30, 52
Dynamics 75, 80–81, 91

E
Edit 25, 34–35, 46–47, 50, 55
Edit button 25, 50, 54
Edit links 48, 51
Edit mode 25, 51
Editing 28, 34, 48, 51–52, 73
Ellipses 31, 39, 59, 78
Email 6, 31, 33, 59, 88, 91
Embed code functionality of SharePoint 52
Embed tab 52–53
Embedded document 53–54
Enterprise levels 1
Environments 1, 11, 34, 40–41
Error 68, 80, 91
Excel 18–19, 34, 57, 60, 80
Excel web access 57
Export 18–19, 60
External systems 63, 75
External users 4, 6–8
External users licensing 4–5

F
File Share 12–13
Files 14–15, 30, 33–35, 43, 70, 75, 79, 81–83, 85–86
– new 75, 77
Finish button 46, 66
Flow 22, 75–90, 92
– standard 34
Flow condition 80
Flow history 82
Flow interface 89
Flow page 90
Flow process 82–83
Flow step 78
Flow templates 75–77
Flow website 84
Flow window 85, 87
Folder 13–15, 30, 33–34, 85–86
– local 33
Functional web part 62
Functionality 10, 12, 29, 32, 34, 37, 50, 52, 54
– complex 62–63
– extensive 12, 40
– workflow 75, 89

G
GetQuote 68, 71
Guest access 4–5
Guest users 4
– external 4

H
Hero web part 46–48
– default 47
Home page 4, 43, 54–55
Home tab 24, 38
Host web 65–66

I
Icon-bar 71
Images 24, 29, 47, 52
Information 8, 10–12, 15, 20–21, 23–24, 26, 28, 81, 87
– contact 26–27
Integrations 60, 91
Invitations 4, 6–7, 12
– external user email 6

J, K
JavaScript 61, 70
JQuery files 67, 70
JSON 68–70

L
Landing page 47
Layouts 43–45, 51–52, 60
Level 1, 5, 20–21, 35, 61, 74
Libraries 14, 17, 24, 31, 38, 85–86
– destination document 14
– target document 14
Licensed O365 users 4
Licenses 1–4, 90
– purchase 4
Licensing 1–4, 6, 8, 10, 12, 14, 16, 18, 20
Limitations 43, 60, 75, 92
Links 6, 8, 18–19, 23, 35, 47–49, 52, 56–57, 59
Listing 67–70
Lists, new 26–27
Local active directory users 8
Lock 33–34
Log 1, 6, 20, 47, 60, 81

M
Managing flows 89
Menu 22, 33, 79
– drop-down 5, 14, 28, 31
Microsoft Flow 2, 75, 77, 84, 89, 91
Microsoft forms 57, 60
Microsoft forms for surveys 57, 59
Microsoft SharePoint 75
Migrating documents 12
Migration 12, 14
Migration tool 14–15
Modifying pages 50–51

N
Name 23, 26–27, 29, 44, 48, 62, 66, 79, 81–82
Navbar 71
Navigate 4, 21, 23, 47
Navigation 23, 48–50
Navigation bar 23, 29, 49
Navigation menu, site's 29
Notification 14, 31, 33, 87, 90–91

O
Objects 35, 37
Office 1–3, 7, 9, 12, 34
Office/SharePoint option 65
OneDrive 33
Online version 34, 43, 64
On-premise SharePoint instances 12

P
Package, jQuery 66–67
Page, new 30, 65
Page.aspx file 70
Parent site 5, 23–24
Permission level 5, 35
Permissions 2, 4–5, 14, 20, 23, 32, 35, 37, 87
Permissions screen 36
Power BI 2, 56
Power BI control 56
Preview 10–11, 53, 59
Preview admin center 10
Process 72, 75, 84, 90
– configure workflow 75

Q
Question type 58
Quick launch 48–49

R
Reports 9–11, 14, 16–20, 56–57, 90
– audit 17–18
Request 4, 88
Right corner, upper 5, 7, 24–25, 35, 54, 59, 85, 87
Roll-up 3, 11

S
Screen 4, 7, 17–18, 22, 24, 44–45, 48–49, 52, 89–90
Script section 70
Script src 70–71
Scripts 67, 70–71
Settings icon 5, 16, 22, 24–25, 38–39, 43–44
Share button 6, 35–36
Share tab 36, 59
Shared documents 78
SharePoint 1, 9–12, 18–19, 32–34, 50–54, 60–64, 70–73, 81–82, 84–85

– accessing 15
– administrating 10
– customize 50
SharePoint add-in 63
SharePoint admin center 21
SharePoint administration 9, 11
SharePoint administration functionality 9
SharePoint client-side solution generator 61
SharePoint component types 21
SharePoint components 62, 74
SharePoint content approval 85
SharePoint deployments, large 12
SharePoint environment 11, 21
SharePoint function 34
SharePoint implementations 12, 38
SharePoint infrastructure 20
SharePoint instance 20
SharePoint instance set 1
SharePoint library 33
SharePoint lists 57
SharePoint migration tool 12
SharePoint online 2, 4, 9, 12, 14, 34, 60, 64, 89
SharePoint online instance 1
SharePoint online sites 43
SharePoint on-premise implementation 43
SharePoint option 45
SharePoint settings option 4
SharePoint site, basic 41
SharePoint sites 4, 19, 29, 44, 47, 63
SharePoint site's layout 61
SharePoint URLs, internal 49
Sharepoint.com 14
SharePoint-hosted option 63
Signatures 76, 87
Site
– active 10–11, 16
– multiple 12, 22
Site contents page 24, 39
Site name 45–46
Site pages 12, 45, 48, 51
Site permissions 4–5, 36
Site settings 5, 16–18, 22, 36, 48–49, 89
Site settings page 4, 19, 49
Site template 45–46
Span class 71
Start 45, 52–53, 56–57, 62, 75, 78, 87
String 27, 81

Styling 43
Styling and visuals 43–44, 46, 48, 50, 52, 54, 56, 58, 60
Subscription 1, 12
Subsite 5, 16, 21–24, 36, 39, 44, 49
– new 22–23
Subsite level 23
Subsite page 25, 38
Sync 33–34
Sync document libraries 33

T
Tab 8, 12, 14, 27, 29, 36–37, 50, 52, 54
– new 21–22
Tasks 38–40
– list of 38–39
Tbody 68
Td 68
Templates 23, 43, 45, 47, 76, 84–85, 87
– new 84, 92
– visual 43
– workflow 84
Test 61–62, 73, 82, 84, 87
Test button 82, 84
Text 29, 31, 51, 58, 71, 81, 91
Thead 71
Tiles 46–48
Timeline 39–40
Toolbar 8, 31, 33, 50, 52, 73
Tools 4, 12, 29, 41, 60–61, 75, 88, 91
Top Link Bar 48–49
Try the preview tab 10
Type 5, 27, 29, 57, 62, 70–71, 74
Type SharePoint add-in 62

U
Update 5, 49
Uploaded documents 32
URL 11, 14, 22–23, 29–30, 48, 68–70, 72
– base 21, 45
Usage reports 15, 17, 19
User administration 7
Users 1–2, 4, 6–8, 12, 14–15, 32–33, 35, 37–39, 46–47
– business 75
– multiple 30, 34
– new 2, 81
Users tab 2

V
Version history 33
Visual Studio 61–62, 65–66, 73
Visual Studio Windows application 62
Visuals 43–44, 46, 48, 50, 52, 54, 56, 58, 60

W, X, Y, Z
Web pages 24, 26
– custom 29
Web part 43, 46, 52, 57, 60–63, 65, 67–68,
    70, 72–74
– custom 29, 52, 61, 74
– final 57, 65
Web part code 62, 67, 69, 71, 73
Web part developers 61
Web part development 62

Web part framework 62
Web part icon 56
Web parts
– adding 26
– standard 60–61
Window 5, 12, 21–22, 29, 32, 53, 57, 65,
    76–77
Word 32, 34
Word documents 12, 34, 52
Word online 32, 52–53
Workflow requirements 92
Workflow settings tab 89
Workflows 41, 75–78, 80, 82, 84, 86–92
– legacy 89
www.alphavantage.co/query 68–69